THE HOPE
OF THE GOSPEL

*Theological Education and
the Next Evangelicalism*

Mark S. Young

WILLIAM B. EERDMANS PUBLISHING COMPANY

GRAND RAPIDS, MICHIGAN

Wm. B. Eerdmans Publishing Co.
4035 Park East Court SE, Grand Rapids, Michigan 49546
www.eerdmans.com

28 27 26 25 24 23 22   1 2 3 4 5 6 7

ISBN 978-0-8028-7886-1

Library of Congress Cataloging-in-Publication Data

Names: Young, Mark, 1956– author.
Title: The hope of the gospel : theological education and the next
    evangelicalism / Mark S. Young.
Description: Grand Rapids : Wm. B. Eerdmans Publishing Co., 2022.
    | Series: Theological education between the times | Includes bib-
    liographical references. | Summary: "A call for evangelical semi-
    naries to renew their commitment to the centrality of the gospel
    so that the evangelical movement might become a more credible
    and compelling Christlike witness for the sake of the world"—
    Provided by publisher.
Identifiers: LCCN 2021029609 | ISBN 9780802878861
Subjects: LCSH: Theological seminaries. | Evangelicalism.
Classification: LCC BV4020 .Y68 2022 | DDC 230.071/1—dc23
LC record available at https://lccn.loc.gov/2021029609

THE HOPE OF THE GOSPEL

THEOLOGICAL EDUCATION BETWEEN THE TIMES

Ted A. Smith, series editor

Theological Education between the Times gathers diverse groups of people for critical, theological conversations about the meanings and purposes of theological education in a time of deep change. The project is funded by the Lilly Endowment Inc.

To Dad
because the past matters

and to Ben, Bonnie, and Christian
because the future matters more

Contents

CONTENTS

Preface

I still believe in theological education. And I've been at it a long time. Now, more than ever, I believe that personally meaningful, richly spiritual, powerfully formative, prophetically courageous, and missionally focused theological education is absolutely necessary for the church to thrive in the future. I also believe that the way we evangelicals think about and do theological education today isn't going to meet that need.

This book flows from deep gratitude for the privilege of being a theological educator for more than four decades. Seeing lives transformed in the classroom transform the lives of others gives me a profound sense of fulfillment. From the classroom to the boardroom, I've loved being a theological educator.

But this book also comes from a place of uneasiness about the future of evangelical theological education. It likely betrays the weight of wondering if evangelical seminaries can become what they need to be to help evangelicalism become what it claims it wants to be.

But I still believe in the enterprise. And I'm hopeful.

This book is written for a group of young leaders who will shape evangelical theological education in the decades to come. These leaders are early in their careers and are already playing significant roles in their respective schools. Moreover, each represents many other young leaders in evangelical schools and churches whom I've met in recent years.

Anna is an articulate and ambitious leader who isn't afraid of pursuing big goals and is willing to pay a high price to attain them. She is creative, data-driven, and strategic in her thinking. Impatient with inefficiencies in systems and processes, she goes where others fear to tread to make things better, even if it raises the hackles of departmental gatekeepers. Raised and schooled in white conservative settings, she is finding her voice and her stride as a woman in the male-dominated evangelical subculture. She will have to navigate the slights, misperceived motives, and entrenched stereotypes of that culture to continue contributing at the level her strengths portend. She has more upside in her future than she knows. Anna believes in the importance of theological education for the church and for the world.

Justin leads a multiracial congregation in a gentrifying urban neighborhood. An insightful and critical thinker, he has learned to navigate the intricacies of being an African American man in predominately white institutional settings. He has done so without losing his prophetic voice in the constant struggle to create spaces where black voices must be heard. By identifying with evangelicalism, he has paid the price of being misunderstood by many in both the black and white communities. And he is making a difference in both. Justin loves learning so much that he has been willing to come back to an institution that hurt him deeply in order to complete two graduate degrees. He is pursuing PhD studies and aspires to be a scholar-pastor who contributes in academic and ecclesial settings. Justin believes that theological education must address the questions, objections, and skepticism of those who don't see the church as the answer to much of anything.

Ellie is a brilliant young scholar and theologian. Although discouraged from pursuing theological training by her pastor in a conservative, predominately white evangelical church, she has persevered. Ellie's drive, tenacity, and raw talent have allowed her to complete multiple master's degrees and enter a PhD program at a prestigious American university. Her scholarship is impeccable, her compassion for the hurting genuine, and her commitment to the church unwavering. She believes in theological education's power to change the way evangelicals address the complexities of contemporary society and bring healing through the power of the gospel.

Brett, a faculty member and midlevel administrator, is completing his PhD, teaching, publishing, and carrying administrative responsibilities while he and his wife raise young children and struggle to make ends meet. He models the oft-impossible balancing act of scholarship, teaching, administration, and financial stress that many future faculty members will face in undercapitalized, tuition-driven evangelical schools. When it comes to innovation, Brett is generally two steps ahead of most administrative and faculty leaders. He is learning how to navigate institutional governance dynamics and structures to bring about change that the institution doesn't yet see that it needs. And he is patient enough to wait for that change to come. Brett believes that theological education *must* change in order to convince a skeptical church of its relevance.

Sofia lives with a passion for her people. A "Dreamer" whose parents brought her to the United States as a child, she navigates the linguistic and cultural differences between her beloved Hispanic culture and the predominately white Anglo culture of most evangelical theological schools. The vibrant, expressive, life-giving faith of her Pentecostal roots doesn't seem to have a seat at the table of most evangelical theologies. She craves a living theology for the streets, one that does not look away from systemic racism, ethnocentrism, gross economic disparities, unjust labor practices, and immoral immigration policies. She believes evangelical theological education has lost its prophetic voice in our culture, and she will not stop advocating for those whose voices are absent in evangelical seminaries.

Five young leaders.[1] Five believers in theological education. Five evangelicals from whom the church needs to hear more than it knows or is willing to admit. Each is dear to me. They represent a growing cohort of reformers who, if afforded the personal, financial, and institutional support they need, will shape theological education for the next evangelicalism. This book is for them.

The challenges facing evangelical theological schools are daunting. The more urgent ones, like paying the bills, capture our attention far more readily than those that lie latent in the assumptions and values of our institutions. In the near term, the leaders of these institutions will wake up nearly every day wondering if they can create a sustainable financial model for tuition-driven schools. That's the harsh reality for most evangelical seminaries. We will use our gifts innovatively to deliver theological education in ways that more people can access. Some of our ideas will work; many won't.

But this book isn't about meeting the need for changes in the institutional and financial models of evangelical theological education. The leaders of most evangelical schools are clever enough and committed enough to figure out how to help their institutions survive and, in some cases, even thrive, in spite of the challenges we face.

This book is about how the assumptions, commitments, and values we are inheriting as evangelical theological educators need to be rethought and recalibrated for the future. It's about the need for evangelicals to carve out the next evangelicalism,[2] one that truly makes the hope of the gospel the foundation of its identity and mission. It's the book I wish someone had handed me forty years ago.

Acknowledgments

Far too rarely, it seems, we give ourselves permission to step out of the fray and just think. Rarer still are opportunities to do so around a table graced by the presence of brothers and sisters in Christ whose keen minds and generous spirits inspire, comfort, and grant courage to all present. Through the generosity of the Lilly Foundation and the vision of Ted Smith, such was the table set for twelve theological educators from dramatically diverse backgrounds and institutions. I am deeply grateful for each of them and for the times we shared around that table.

Gifted colleagues, committed donors, wise trustees, and passionate students all contribute to the character and mission of a theological seminary and to the deeply satisfying life of being a theological educator. I am thankful for the way the truly remarkable community of Jesus followers at Denver Seminary has formed, challenged, encouraged, and sustained me through the past twelve years.

How does a kid who grew up in a small town in Appalachia end up in places like Moscow, Maputo, and Mumbai exercising his gifts and passion as a theological educator? How does he have the joy of breaking bread with Muslims, animists, Hindus, Buddhists, atheists, and skeptics who have given their lives to Christ? Only by the generosity of our gracious God. For that generosity and that grace I am truly thankful. I stand amazed in the Presence.

– What Matters –

Dear Anna, Justin, Ellie, Brett, and Sofia,

Leading a theological seminary is first and foremost a theological task. A school's mission and vision—those bedrock questions upon which institutional forms, operational strategies, and academic programs are built—must be formulated on the basis of shared theological convictions about the nature of God's mission in the world, the role of God's people in that mission, and the unique contribution theological education can make to that mission.

Therefore, don't forget to think. For those of us who dare to take a leadership role in a theological school, it's a surprisingly easy thing to forget. Administrative duties and personnel crises devour everything in their path, including our attention, our heart, and our time. That's why you must make time to shut down the computer, turn off the phone, shove the papers on the desk aside, and ask yourself one question: "What matters most to me as a theological educator?" Fight your educator's bent to critique the answer. Don't wordsmith it; just write it down. And think about it. Why is that your first answer? What longing in your soul does it express? What deeply valued convictions flow from it? How do your teaching and leadership express what matters most to you?

And don't forget to hope. Institutional and operational matters can smother hope and cloud vision. But hope centers our faith and *our calling as educators, for both the gospel and education promise a future better than the present. Hope drives students to undertake the arduous process of transformation and compels us to journey with them toward their desired and envisioned future. In like manner, hope makes the power of the gospel immanent. It urges us to lean into our faith in Christ even when doing so seems to make little sense. The hope of the gospel gives meaning to life in a world that wobbles on a thin ledge above the twin hells of nihilism and hedonism.*

Because the gospel matters, theological education matters. What a privilege to give our lives to both.

Grateful for you,
Mark

1

The Hope of the Gospel

Evangelicalism builds its brand promise on hope. With a gospel message that envisions a better life on this earth and in heaven, the heart of evangelical religious experience and theology beats with hope.

The power of hope lies in its ability to help us navigate present circumstances with a vision of a better future. It fills the gap in our souls between what is true now and what we want to be true in the future. Hope gives us permission to aspire to something better, and it animates us to act in ways that move us closer to that "better."

Hope grounds and drives education. Most adult learners carry an image of a future deemed better than their present and expect education to create a pathway toward the realization of that image. Exemplary teaching informs, equips, and inspires students to keep pursuing their vision of a future they do not currently experience. Such is my personal testimony.

As a child with deep roots in Appalachia, my vision of the future was bounded by a family with no history of higher education and a culture that placed little value on higher education. For so many in that beautiful and culturally rich region, any vision of the future stopped at the rims of the topographical and cultural "hollers" where we lived.

Neither of my parents attended college. My dad was the first in his family to go to high school. At their insistence and with their financial help, however, I attended an underfunded regional public university twenty-five miles from our home. With minimal library holdings, little industry or government funding for research, and no academic reputation to attract and retain top scholars, that university was woefully short on resources. But it was long on hope. For those who dared to envision a future beyond the "holler," it promised a pathway to that end. At that university, I fell in love with learning and surrendered to the power of hope in education. Although I could not see the future, I knew that its contours must include a life of learning, teaching, and instilling hope in the lives of those who dared to envision a future different from their present.

During those years, I also strengthened my faith in Christ and fervently embraced the hope of the gospel. Whereas education helped form a vision of my personal future, the gospel of Christ gave me a vision of a cosmic future. Looking back on those years, I have no doubt that I made a lifelong faith commitment to both education and the gospel because they both touched the deep chord of hope residing in my soul. Both promised a better future for me personally, and both demanded of me the pursuit of a better future for others. Hope spawned a dual calling as educator and minister of the gospel that has defined me for over forty years. That's why hope frames my understanding of the identity and mission of evangelical theological education.

As the title of this series of books—Theological Education between the Times—captures so well, theological education in North America faces realities that cry out for dramatic change. Evangelical theological education is not immune to those realities. In fact, evangelical schools are driving the pace of change that characterizes much of Protestant theological education in North America today.

Change is not new in theological education. Institutional forms and educational practice have been adapted to new contextual realities throughout the years, sometimes with a modicum of pace but more frequently at glacial speed. Glacial speed won't work anymore. A sense of urgency drives most of the change in theological schools today. It comes from the sincere concern that many schools simply will not survive, much less fulfill their historical mission, unless they change in ways that increase enrollment. Evangelical theological schools are especially vulnerable to this threat. Although in the fall of 2020 around 70 percent of students enrolled in ATS-accredited institutions attended an evangelical seminary, many evangelical schools have experienced declining enrollment and tuition revenue over the previous decade. Since the majority of evangelical schools lack sufficient long-term investments to fund operations without increasing tuition revenue, they have been forced to make dramatic changes to program content and delivery, marketing and recruitment strategies, and faculty roles and responsibilities. A fellow evangelical seminary president described the last five years as a period of "frenzied change."

I sometimes fear that change has become an idol for theological educators, a twenty-first-century Molech (Jer. 32:35) that promises more than it delivers and demands more than it gives in return. Instead of being linear, organized, and progressive, change is often serpentine, frequently messy, and sometimes regressive. Change is not theological education's deliverer, but it must be an educator's constant companion and conversation partner. It is not worthy of our adoration, but it does demand our attention. Though institutional change will not meet all the challenges we face, it may assuage our fears for a while (and keep the doors open and the lights on). Evangelical theological education needs more than change: it needs a refocused *raison d'être*, a calling, a mission.

Theological education is first and foremost a theological enterprise. Whether explicitly or tacitly, a community's shared theological convictions shape the vision, strategies, structures, and practices of theological education. We evangelicals might be tempted to think that while educational models and modes must change, our theological convictions must remain unchanged.

However, as a human enterprise, nothing about theological education is immune to the need for change, including the ways we formulate and express our theology. It would be naïve to assert otherwise.

The shared theological convictions that imbue our educational practice and forms are not necessarily found in the formal creeds, confessions, and doctrinal statements that undergird our form of identity politics. Theological grounding for educational practice is seldom accomplished through communal reaffirmations of a confessional statement, no matter how tightly formulated and policed such doctrinal compliance may be by institutional governance, denominational authorities, and constituent dollars. That's not to say that such formal statements are irrelevant. Indeed, they are an evangelical school's bona fides. Moreover, they often shape the school's curricular content, program structures, and educational resourcing, particularly faculty deployment.

The shared theological convictions that are most formative in shaping educational practice, however, are much more visceral, more instinctual, and more deeply valued than many of the affirmations that make up the theological distinctions and identities of various schools. These convictions are immanent: they bring the eternal into the present. They are incarnate: they usher the transcendent into the gritty realities of human experience. And they must not be undervalued, lest our work become vacant and vapid.

The theological convictions that shape educational practice lie in a community's sense of God's engagement in the world and their participation as God's people in that engagement. The first question theological educators need to ask themselves is, "What theological language connects my understanding of God's purpose and engagement in the world with the present gritty realities of human experience?" And the second, although much less noble-sounding question, is just as important, "When the life-draining financial reports, soul-numbing committee meetings, mind-boggling academic trivialities, and head-shaking institutional pettinesses are momentarily silenced in my heart, *what matters most to me as a theological educator?*" These questions can help us find the "You Are Here" dot on the map of our cluttered minds and souls.

For me, three words always come to mind when I think about those two questions: "gospel," "redemption," and "hope." The *gospel* is "good news" that God has intervened in human history in the person of his Son to address the three enemies that have plagued all of humanity since our unfortunate encounter with the serpent in the garden—sin, death, and evil. That's good news, really good news. *Redemption* describes how God is resolving those three problems. The present brokenness of this world does not remain unchallenged; it will not last forever. Through the life, death, and resurrection of Jesus, God intervenes on humanity's behalf, rescues us from that which holds us in bondage, and restores us to relationship with himself. The good news of redemption brings *hope* to humanity. Hope is the gospel made immanent, incarnate, and certain. It is the experience of God's redemptive engagement in human history in a most intimate, vulnerable, and meaningful way.

Hope is the personal and communal experience of the gospel of redemption that lies at the center of our theology. For theological education to remain evangelical in this time of intense pressure for change in institutional forms and educational practice, the enduring ground and frame of the enterprise must remain the hope of redemption. That's why I believe the identity and mission of evangelical theological education spring from the lived reality and promise of redemption, what the apostle Paul calls "the hope held out in the gospel" (Col. 1:23).[1]

Theological education "between the times" creates space for the unsettling reminder that institutional forms and instructional delivery aren't the only aspects of the enterprise that must change. Even our most important centering theological convictions like the hope of the gospel must be reconceptualized, reformulated, and rearticulated in theological language and religious experience that will speak compellingly to successive generations in the changing cultural and religious landscape of North America.

As parts of a religious movement that seeks both to transform the world and to hold on to what matters most, evangelical schools face a constant tension around questions of change. Whereas adoption of new practices to meet contemporary needs satisfies evangelical sensibilities and helps fulfill the movement's intrinsic impulse to expand, the adoption of new or revised theological language and understanding goes against the grain of a movement that values conformity and continuity with its confessed identity and beliefs. Although an unwelcome companion in many schools, this tension is a *necessary and abiding reality* for the future of evangelical theological education.

The breadth and complexity of evangelical theological education boggle the mind. That breadth has developed because most evangelicals have consistently valued theological training in some form or fashion throughout our history. In addition, deep in the heart of evangelicalism is an entrepreneurial spirit that is animated by a commitment to expansion. "More" is one of our favorite words. Our common yearning is, "More, always more."

These two factors—a value on theological education and an entrepreneurial impulse to expand—have contributed to the creation of a stunning array of educational efforts that operate on every inhabited continent with instruction in hundreds of languages delivered at educational levels that range from preliteracy classes to doctoral seminars. Evangelical theological education operates in formal, informal, and nonformal modes, on campuses, in church buildings, online, and in thousands of living rooms, conference centers, and rented office spaces. Some of these endeavors offer accredited degrees, but the vast majority do not. Multiply the above variables by dozens of denominations, parachurch organizations, accrediting associations, and mission agencies, each with its own ordination, professional development, and curricular requirements. Evangelical theological education, when taken as a whole, is as polymorphous, disjointed, and seemingly chaotic as the movement itself.

No single volume could adequately explore the identity and mission of such a multifaceted enterprise. This work focuses on only a small slice of it, namely, graduate-level, ATS-accredited evangelical institutions of theological education in the United States. Although accounting for a relatively small percentage of the theological education programs operated by evangelicals worldwide, accredited North American seminaries and divinity schools wield disproportionate influence globally on the development and growth of programs and initiatives in theological education. Many of the scholars, leaders, and practitioners in theological education outside the United States have been influenced by accredited evangelical schools in North America.

I write as an insider, someone whose religious identity has been nurtured and shaped by organizations and educational institutions deeply entrenched in the socioreligious movement in the United States known as evangelicalism. I write with gratitude for that personal history and with great affection for the many people within the movement who have cared for and shaped me. In the pages that follow, you will not hear the voice of a disaffected son who has rejected his upbringing and heritage in order to find something better. It's the voice of a concerned son—one who is grateful, sympathetic, critical, and hopeful in equal measure.

Evangelicalism is its "best self" when we remember that we are first and foremost "gospel people"—hope-mongers, not fear-mongers—in the marketplace of competing narratives about what it means to know God as fully and spectacularly flawed human beings. The convictions we hold are far more beautiful and life-giving than the fears we share. The former lead to remarkable virtues that create a compelling vision of the resurrected Christ; the latter lead only to debilitating vices that disgust, repel, and harm those who suffer their consequences. Our shared history is replete with both.

Evangelicalism matters. As the drumbeat for change in our society increases, so does the need for God's people to respond with theologically informed practice and convictions that create a credible and compelling gospel presence. The question before us as theological educators is whether evangelical theological education can be a driving force in helping spawn the next evangelicalism. It can do so only if theological education and the movement are grounded and framed by what really matters: the hope of the gospel.

2

Who Are We?

Over thirty million people have taken DNA tests to gain insight into their personal family histories. Companies that sell these tests promise that you can discover who you *truly* are by exploring your family of origin. By understanding our past better, we hope to understand ourselves better. Learning about our family history can help satisfy the need to belong to something, the need to be connected to something bigger, more transcendent than the immanent and the immediate in our lives. As evangelicals, we are connected to something much bigger than our own personal religious experience. We bear the theological and socioreligious DNA of those who have shaped our movement, and we share it with millions of believers worldwide.

I can't recall ever making a conscious decision to become an evangelical.[1] I was born and raised in a small town in Appalachia and baptized as a child in the church my family had attended for generations. My faith was in Christ and my church was American Baptist. That seemed simple enough. And when my faith commitment was awakened through involvement in a campus ministry and a sense of calling took root in my heart, there was no deep longing to become "an evangelical." In fact, at that time I'm not sure I was even aware of the labels—fundamentalist, evangelical, mainline—that define Protestant Christianity in North America.

I became an evangelical by default, I suppose, by choosing to attend the seminary where one of my favorite conference speakers was a faculty member. I knew nothing about that school's place in the constellation of religious schools. Its fundamentalist roots and instincts, along with its emphasis on biblical literalism and apocalypticism, seemed normative to me and others who chose to be a part of that community. I was an eager learner and soaked up the convictions and values of that institution without being aware that it occupied a rather marginalized conservative place among evangelical seminaries. Because I was formed by this school, my induction into evangelicalism was a *fait accompli.*

Like so many during that era, I became an evangelical and embraced the identity knowing precious little about the history of the movement, its social location in the United States, and its conservative political instincts. I simply desired to be around people who shared my sense of what it meant to follow Jesus: have a testimony of personal faith in the gospel, study the Bible seriously, strive to live in line with its teachings, and share the good news with as many people as possible. It was as simple as that.

Those of us who hitch our wagons to institutions historically aligned with evangelicalism belong to something bigger than our own faith journey. But I'm not sure we know what that something is. Evangelicalism becomes harder to define and defend with each passing year. Frankly, our movement suffers from an acute identity crisis. As historian Molly Worthen writes, "The term evangelical has produced more debate than agreement. The word is so mired in adjectives and qualifiers, contaminated by politicization and stereotype, that many commentators have suggested that it has outlived its usefulness. In America alone, the broad tent of evangelicalism includes a definition-defying array of doctrines, practices, and political persuasions. . . . Yet we are stuck with it."[2]

Stuck with it, indeed. Those outside the movement have settled on a social and political definition of the term that is much more easily observed and measured than the theological meaning insiders prefer. Some have decided they can no longer identify with the movement after a strong majority of their fellow evangelicals uncritically supported Donald Trump in the 2016 and 2020 presidential campaigns. Many of us are trying to convince ourselves and others that evangelicalism hasn't degenerated into being merely a partisan political bloc. But that's tough sledding. Evangelical leaders with broad media exposure unwaveringly defend Trump, explain away patterns of behavior that have nothing in common with what we say matters to us ethically, affirm decisions that contradict traditional evangelical values, and attack fellow evangelicals who dare criticize him. Our participation in the political process has confirmed as true the assumption of the broader culture that evangelical simply means conservative, partisan Republican. The movement that so many of us have called our spiritual home has lost its theological character, its moral compass, its social credibility, and its soul.

The question we need to ask ourselves is painfully clear: "Is it worth holding on to the label 'evangelical'?" That question hovers like threatening storm clouds over the future of evangelical theological education. For now, most of the theological education institutions that have been identified with the movement have retained the moniker, honoring their history, alumni, and constituents. Some of us refuse to surrender an identity that expresses our theological essence, the gospel. Let's not give up on "evangelical" yet. Let's redefine it and remake it. Younger leaders emerging in institutions that historically have been aligned with the movement have an opportunity to carve out the next evangelicalism, just as those who spawned the movement in the early 1940s crafted a new religious identity that distanced itself from the separatist instincts, angry rhetoric, doomsday apocalypticism, and anti-intellectualism of early twentieth-century fundamentalism in the United States.

But we can't carve out the next evangelicalism if we don't first figure out what it means to be an evangelical today. Confusion and disagreement about the terms "evangelical" and "evangelicalism" are not new. Because evangelicalism is unlike any other religious movement in North America, the broader public simply doesn't have categories and labels that do justice to its breadth and complexity. Both outsiders, who prefer to think of evangelical as a primarily political identity, and we insiders, who prefer to think of ourselves in primarily theological terms, have adopted approaches that are unsatisfying and too simplistic to be of much help in understanding the movement that has cut such a wide swath across the religious landscape of the United States.

Perhaps searching for a definition of evangelicalism is folly. As one historian put it, "evangelicalism needs to be relinquished as a religious identity because it does not exist."[3] But it is strange how something that "does not exist" dominates the public conversation about religion in the United States. Over 90 million people in North America self-identify as evangelical, and estimates of the number of evangelicals worldwide exceed 650 million. As a loosely allied constellation of various denominations, churches, academic institutions, media outlets, mission agencies, publishing houses, worship bands, and celebrity preachers, evangelicalism befuddles those who want to compare it to established religious identities with recognized institutional structures. No single person or organization speaks authoritatively for all evangelicals or evangelicalism. Yet somehow, in spite of its dizzying diversity of voices, raucous theological debates, disruptive schisms, and exhausting entrepreneurial impulse, evangelicals have created what one historian calls "the most vital Christian movement on the scene" today.[4]

If we cannot satisfactorily define it, then perhaps describing evangelicalism is a better pathway forward. Like most socioreligious movements, evangelicalism is built upon *shared history*, *shared convictions*, and *shared religious experience*. Even with such diverse constituent groups, evangelicalism has retained throughout its history some remarkably resilient priorities and traits—its theological DNA—that demarcate its identity in the religious landscape of North America. Understanding that resilience has occupied the attention of historians, theologians, social scientists, and journalists for decades.[5] And interest in evangelicalism has only grown in recent years. Publishers, news agencies, and media outlets can't seem to get enough of the drama surrounding evangelicalism and its dalliance with Trump. What an indictment. The broader culture is far more interested in our politics than our gospel because we aren't engaging the public square in a way that makes our gospel more interesting and compelling than our politics.

Our current identity crisis is a self-inflicted wound. We've lost sight of what matters most—the hope of the gospel—in our misguided, quixotic, and idolatrous quest to "win" the culture wars through political ascendancy. Carving out the next evangelicalism will demand that we make what matters most that which most defines us.

– Past Matters –

Dear Justin, Ellie, Brett, Sofia, and Anna,

I grew up in a house built near the beginning of the twentieth century, a "Jenny Lind" house, as we call it in Appalachia, constructed in board and batten style. Originally, it had three rooms: a living room, a bedroom, and a workroom that housed a loom to weave rugs and blankets. The kitchen and outhouse were two separate sheds behind the main house. By the time my parents bought the house in the 1950s, a kitchen had been added to the main structure, running water brought in, and the workroom turned into a bathroom. Through the years, they added a second bedroom, a front porch, and a garage. The foundation of those three original rooms remains in place. All that came after them is ultimately tied to that foundation; it created the limitations and the possibilities for what the house could and would become.

Our history is the foundation that creates both the limitations and possibilities of evangelicalism. Unfortunately, we tend to make two crippling errors in relation to our history. First, we are woefully ignorant of it. We are shaped by a history we do not know in ways we cannot detect. Second, we mistake nostalgia for historical awareness. Many in our movement long to go back and recover the simple faith and way of life they want to believe existed in our past. But nostalgia is not a Christian virtue. Hope is. Evangelical theology calls us to long for the future God has promised, not the past. That promised future far exceeds any romanticized notion of our past.

The better we know our history, the more we may be able to strip away what we want our past to have been and see ourselves as we actually were. A distorted view of our past gives us license to justify a distorted view of our identity and mission in the present. But a fiercely courageous and steely-eyed gaze into our history grounds our understanding of the present in reality. The better we know our history, the more we will be able to help shape our movement into the beautiful hope-filled, gospel-centered presence that the world yearns for but doesn't know where to find.

Hopeful for you,

Mark

3

The DNA of Evangelicalism

The past matters. Our history shapes who we are today. It molds the contours of our boundaries and establishes the baseline for our potential. We dare not dream of the next evangelicalism without a clear-eyed reckoning with the history of our movement.

Most evangelicals have a tortured relationship with their history. Equally valued commitments to biblicism and pragmatism pull us in opposite directions. Looking to the past, we want to believe that our faith today is aligned with that of the first-century churches described in the New Testament. Therefore, "Is it biblical?" rolls off our tongues instinctively. We use that question as a foundation for understanding how to think and act as followers of Christ. On the other hand, we crave personal benefit and success from our faith today as an assurance that what we believe is true. As a result, "Does it work?" comes in a close second to "Is it biblical?" when we consider questions of faith and practice. In the absence of formal ecclesiastical and theological authority structures, we use these two questions to validate the way we frame our beliefs and shape our practices in the present. Although we are hesitant to admit it because of the preeminent role biblicism plays in the hierarchy of our convictions, our pragmatism betrays the reality that we see both questions as equally authoritative.

Biblicism and pragmatism as twin values create a troubling ahistorical approach to faith that downplays the influence of two thousand years of historical and cultural distance between

19

the first-century world of the New Testament and our twenty-first-century North American context. Evangelicals want to believe we can fly back and forth between these two historically and culturally distant coastlines with little regard for what lies below the flight path. We treat our history like flyover country. As a result, our faith is shaped in ways we do not recognize by a history we do not know. The psychological and social need to be convinced that what we believe and how we behave are derived directly from an accurate interpretation of the Bible simply does not allow us to admit fully that our hermeneutics, theology, and practice are shaped as much by our history and context as by the Bible. Simply put, most of us are ignorant of the history that has shaped us. But shape us it has, and our failure to identify how it has shaped us continues to bedevil and cripple the movement.

Evangelicalism is revivalist religion, a socioreligious renewal movement spawned and energized through recurring reactions to alleged theological error, spiritual malaise, and ecclesiastical failure. It thrives in the constant tension between the need for ordered religious thought and the impulse to seek a more vibrant and more satisfying faith experience. This quest is grounded in our instinct to look back to the Bible to determine what our faith ought to be, to look around and assess whether our current faith experience matches that found in the Bible, and to look ahead so that we can devise ways to recover that "ought" and revitalize the faithful. The impulse to spawn spiritual renewal within the church and the community is deeply embedded in our movement's DNA.

As a revivalist movement, we are reactionaries, shaping our identity in contrast to the established religious traditions and institutions we deem to be in need of renewal. We can frame our history through five significant socioreligious revivalist and renewal movements in Europe and North America: (1) the Protestant Reformation as a reaction against medieval Roman Catholicism, (2) Puritanism and Pietism as a reaction against post-Reformation state church Protestantism, (3) the Great

Awakenings as a reaction to the patchwork of established churches of colonial Protestantism, (4) fundamentalism as a reaction to naturalism and modernism in late nineteenth-century and early twentieth-century Protestantism, and (5) neo-evangelicalism as a reaction to fundamentalism. The next evangelicalism also springs from a vision for renewal, carving out a new identity in reaction to the way the movement has created a parody of itself in the public square for the last fifty years and sold its soul to the twin idols of political power and celebrityism. The next evangelicalism will not silence its prophetic voice nor blur its gospel focus with the naked pursuit of power, wealth, and fame.

Through our shared history the DNA of evangelicalism—our shared convictions and shared religious experience—has developed. The next evangelicalism can ill afford to ignore how this history has shaped our theological instincts, hermeneutical method, and ministerial practice. We cannot envision theological education that will shape the next evangelicalism without reckoning with our past.

We like to define ourselves by what we say we believe. That's a dicey proposition for a movement as diverse as evangelicalism. Yet, drilling through layers of denominational and doctrinal differences, we can find a resilient core of theological and experiential priorities that provide the movement with a measure of coherence and cohesion.

Historian David Bebbington crafted the most commonly used list of theological priorities that characterize evangelicalism—conversionism, activism, biblicism, and crucicentrism. He writes, "There are . . . four qualities that have been the special marks of Evangelical religion: *conversionism*, the belief that lives need to be changed; *activism*, the expression of the gospel in effort; *biblicism*, a particular regard for the Bible; and what may be called *crucicentrism*, a stress on the sacrifice of Christ on the cross. Together they form a quadrilateral of priorities that is the basis of Evangelicalism."[1]

Mark Noll provides a good summary of how these convictions have become universally accepted by evangelicals.

> We [evangelicals] have insisted on the need for a personal relationship to Christ in response to a more "nominal" form of Christianity—as well as over against a "many roads to heaven" relativism. We have proclaimed the supremacy of the Bible's authority as over against those who allow churchly authority to "correct," or to supplement in relativizing ways, the clear teachings of the Scriptures. The centrality of the work of the cross has been a non-negotiable undergirding of the call to sinners to trust in Christ alone as the heaven-sent Savior. And our brand of activism has been our way of insisting that a genuine faith must take shape in the kind of holy living that requires us to bear witness to God's revealed will for our daily lives.[2]

Noll's summary rings true in my own life. I can still hear the revival preacher calling us to turn from our sinful ways in order to find God and be born again (conversionism). The promise of a better life, both now and in the future, has always been a hallmark of evangelical preaching. The death of Christ is the centerpiece of our faith, indeed, the centerpiece of all human history. Only through the shedding of blood could God's wrath be satisfied and our sins forgiven (crucicentrism). We weep over the cruelty of the cross and look beyond it to the resurrection. The Bible holds the key to finding the better life promised by our salvation (biblicism). We study the Bible, memorize it, and weaponize it against those who dare disagree with our interpretation of it. We look to the Bible as the arbiter of truth and the guide for a righteous and happy life. And of course, we want to share this good news with everyone (activism). God's love for us spurs us to acts of love for others so that they can see the gospel in their midst. Yes, those four priorities ring true to the experience of millions of evangelicals.

In and of themselves, these four convictions are not the exclusive purview of evangelicalism. Many Christians around the world who do not identify with the movement claim agreement, if not allegiance, to these beliefs. Yet the role these convictions have played in our history sets evangelicalism apart from other Christian identities. Rich Mouw describes these four tenets as evangelical "emphases that have a lot of history attached to them . . . lines in the past we have drawn in the sand in the midst of specific controversies."[3] Our history with these four priorities—the battles we've fought and the boundaries we've staked out culturally, intellectually, theologically, emotionally, morally, socially, and relationally around them—sets the movement apart from other Protestant expressions of Christian faith. We not only believe them, we also value them. We've paid a heavy price for these priorities, and most of us cannot imagine evangelicalism without them. Nor can we imagine evangelical theological education that isn't characterized by them.

We have to face the disturbing reality, however, that our confession of these shared convictions has not prevented the current identity crisis in evangelicalism. The way we understand and articulate them has failed to shape us into a people known primarily for them. The way we engage the public square has rendered us moot at best, dangerous at worst, and scarcely intelligible to those outside the movement and to the growing number of people who were raised in evangelical families but now find themselves theologically and religiously "homeless." Theological education for the next evangelicalism must challenge us to reconceptualize our theological DNA, rearticulate it for a new generation, and reconsider how to live it out in ways that emphasize the hope of the gospel above all other concerns.

The next evangelicalism will not be created *ex nihilo*. Rather, it will spring from the fertile soil of careful inquiry and critical assessment of how our history has shaped us. In other words, our past matters.

4

The Foundation and Fragmentation
of Faith

Like the beloved family pet of my childhood, evangelicals are of mixed lineage. We are theological mutts shaped by different streams of Christian belief and practice into diverse expressions of faith, worship, and piety. Yet we have enough in common to create a shared identity, an identity that flows from our shared history. Theological education that will help shape the next evangelicalism must take stock of that history in every discipline of study, recognizing its influence, limitations, and benefit in grounding our identity and witness in the hope of the gospel.

We do not lack for credible, expansive, and insightful expositions of the history of evangelicalism.[1] The question is whether we take advantage of these wonderful gifts. Unfortunately, the history of our movement is seldom thoughtfully explored in our pulpits and often cut out of our seminaries' curricula with the demand for shorter, more praxis-oriented degrees in tuition-driven schools. On both counts, that is to our loss. The past matters. To begin formulating a vision for theological education and the next evangelicalism, we need to identify in broad strokes how our history has helped shape the current state of our movement, including our crisis of identity and witness, and how it can provide guidance for carving out more definitively the next iteration of evangelicalism.

As we look to our past, however, we must be careful to avoid the all-too-common posture of harshly judging those who shaped our history with the self-righteousness that earned Jesus's strongest condemnation.[2] What a pathetic way to help ourselves feel better about ourselves. Honesty and humility must define our posture in reflecting on our own history. We gain nothing by overlooking either the virtues or the vices of those who have helped define evangelicalism in the past. And without stepping back from the hard stop between right and wrong, moral and immoral, and just and unjust established in the very character of God, we must interpret their motives and actions, giving credence to the power of the mores of their eras. In like manner, we must humbly acknowledge that in the years ahead, those who come after us will have ample reason to harshly judge what we have done in the name of Christ because of our own blind spots and foibles. After all, we are, like those who came before us and those who will come after us, a hot mess of inconsistencies and contradictions.

The Reformation

American evangelicalism finds its cultural, religious, and theological heritage in northern European history and culture. Although many historians would observe that evangelicalism as a distinct expression of Protestant Christianity does not emerge until the nineteenth century, the Reformation looms large in our historical imagination as the foundation of the movement. For most, it is the "Start Here" dot on the map of our history.

We are theological heirs of a tumultuous sixteenth-century struggle over questions of eternal salvation, religious authority, and the relationship between ecclesiastical and state power. We prefer viewing the Reformation solely through a theological lens, but we must not overlook the pastoral, social, economic, and political concerns energizing the theological inquiry and ecclesiastical dissent that challenged the presence, power, and practice of Roman Catholicism in medieval Europe. Our identity as a renewal and revivalist movement springs from the fertile soil of the Reformers' desire to recover the gospel, renew the church, and set people free from a corrupt, oppressive, and spiritually malignant hierarchy.

"Evangelicals are gospel people."[3] Our very name comes into English from the Greek word *euangelion* ("good news" or "gospel") through the German term *evangelisch*. Martin Luther and other early Reformers used the German phrase *evangelische Kirche* to describe those churches that were no longer a part of the Roman Catholic Church. Essentially, *evangelisch* functioned as a synonym for all Protestants in German-speaking countries. Luther and his fellow Reformers chose the term to emphasize that they, in reaction to the theology and practice of medieval Roman Catholicism in central Europe, had recentered theology on the gospel message as they saw it articulated in the New Testament.

Today, evangelicals find their theological moorings in the Protestant Reformation's *solae* formulations—*sola gratia*, *sola fide*, *solus Christus*.[4] These form the essence of our gospel. They embody our conviction that a person is saved by grace alone through faith alone in Christ alone. These formulations focus our attention on the death of Christ on the cross as the great redemptive act of God through which salvation is accomplished. They create the theological language by which crucicentrism and conversionism become core convictions in our theological DNA. We are, first and foremost, gospel people. At least we like to say we are.

Evangelicals also claim an inheritance from the Reformers' insistence that no sociopolitical or socioreligious institutions, traditions, and theologies may be placed above the authority of Scripture (*sola Scriptura*). The idea of a renewal movement arising through the recovery of plain biblical truth that has been lost, diminished, or hidden by established religious institutions and traditions occupies a powerful place, both intellectually and emotionally, in evangelical self-consciousness up to this day. It is the dais from which biblicism finds its voice at the center of the movement. Biblicism imbues evangelical hermeneutics, teaching, and preaching with a form of religious authority that is deemed more credible than theological tradition and ecclesial dicta. Applying the mantle "biblical" to an idea, a value, or a behavior makes it right, good, and absolute for many evangelicals because, thereby, it is deemed to carry divine authority.

Biblicism has created an ongoing tension for evangelicals around questions of intellectual, theological, and ecclesiastical authority. As the Reformers cast off the authority of the papacy, they thought they were enthroning the Bible in the pope's place. But they weren't. Although we like to claim that the Bible is our final authority in all matters of faith and practice, that has never truly been the case. Humans mediate the authority of the Bible through their interpretation of it. By dethroning the Roman pope as the arbiter of correct doctrine and biblical interpretation, the Reformation lays the groundwork for installing a pope in every evangelical pulpit as the movement comes into its own three centuries hence in the fertile soil of American individualism. The question of authority, although played out somewhat differently in the succeeding revivals and renewals that form the framework for evangelical history, has been the movement's constant companion and torment. And it is still clearly evident in our fractious hermeneutical, theological, political, and ministerial debates today.[5]

Because we like to define ourselves primarily theologically, evangelicals tend to stress the theological developments of the Reformation at the expense of a serious consideration of the economic, social, and political dynamics that led to the creation of Protestant state churches in northern continental Europe, Scandinavia, England, and Scotland. Neither Luther nor Calvin moved away from the need to wed religious and political authority in creating social order and sustaining the common good. Long after the early leaders of the Reformation had died, the political and religious landscape of continental Europe and the British Isles remained in turmoil. Shifting religious allegiances across ethnic, linguistic, and regional lines grew out of the social and political realities of a still-intertwined church and state. The antipathy of Protestants toward Roman Catholicism went far beyond theological questions of salvation, purgatory, and indulgences. It led to war.[6]

Unfortunately, evangelicalism inherited from the Reformation a deeply entrenched anti-Catholic sentiment that has reared its ugly head throughout our history. Although that animosity has been mitigated in the last fifty years in the United States,[7] from the colonial era until the last decade of the twentieth century, many evangelicals in America viewed Roman Catholicism "not as an alternative Christian religion but as the world's most perverse threat to genuine faith."[8]

The fragmentation of Protestantism along doctrinal, ethnic, and political fault lines after the Reformation led to the competing confessional statements, ethno-religious identities, and ecclesiastical institutions from which different strands of evangelicalism in North America would emerge. This fragmentation spawned heresy trials and no small amount of religious, socio-ethnic, and political conflict in northern Europe and Britain. "In this period, as in other premodern societies, it was difficult for most people to distinguish religious from political allegiances. Politics were never absent from theological controversies."[9] Evangelicalism's roots in the Reformation are more politically stained and bloodier than most of us care to admit. Political engagement has always been a part of evangelicalism.

The movement that would become the American version of evangelicalism still bears scars from the turmoil spawned by the dissolution of the Holy Roman Empire and the fragmentation of Protestantism. Our history is inextricably intertwined with an uncertainty about how creedal authority and ecclesiastical identity relate to political authority and state allegiance. Our understanding of the theological foundation we inherited from the Reformation has not created for us a cohesive vision of the relationship of church and state, much less a unified approach to politics and the public square. Neither has it inhibited the tenacity and ferocity of the intramural debates and disputes created by competing evangelical theologies, institutions, and sociopolitical allegiances.

Whereas the *solae* of the Reformation were not understood expansively and humbly enough to prevent the fragmentation of

Protestantism, they were common threads that created the possibility of a religious identity built on shared beliefs and values that could encompass ethno-linguistic, national, cultural, and ecclesiastical diversity. Evangelicalism is the heir of that legacy. As a result, we have consistently demonstrated the capacity to transcend and accommodate diverse approaches to the development and character of theological traditions, confessional statements, and religious institutions, including theological schools and seminaries, while claiming a common theological heritage and religious identity. Like large families, we squabble incessantly but somehow manage to find enough in common to maintain a shared identity. We just don't know who might try to disinherit us at any given time for alleged doctrinal, hermeneutical, and now, political deviations.

The core theological convictions of evangelicalism are grounded in the Reformation. Their power in our movement is unquestioned; they shape the way we see God, ourselves, the world, and salvation. But theology isn't all that we inherited from the Reformation. Antipapist sentiment, schismatic propensities, and the never-ending struggle to figure out the sources of authority in our movement are a part of that legacy as well. Broader cultural assumptions of sixteenth-to-eighteenth-century Europe also reside in our inheritance from the Reformation. Assumptions of white supremacy, seen in the divine right to colonize new lands and take possession of them,[10] and patriarchy are present with us today as a part of our Reformation legacy. Although theological formulations about the dignity of humans and the redemptive work of Christ were voiced in universal terms, these did not change dominant assumptions about race and gender held by the Reformers. American evangelicalism still struggles with them as well. We remain a predominantly white movement with predominantly male leadership. Theological education for the next evangelicalism must challenge the movement to reconsider these deeply held assumptions and critically assess how they shape our values and practices.

Puritanism and Pietism

Reform movements cannot sustain themselves without the development of institutions through which religious identity, community, confession, and practice are perpetuated. But the institutionalization of religious identity and experience ultimately robs the movement of its dynamism. Institutions are designed to conserve and stabilize the hope and energy of the renewal movements from which they spring. But they do the opposite. It is not surprising, therefore, that within a relatively short time, the Reformers created the kinds of institutional religious authority structures and formalism that rekindled the spiritual malaise and abusive power dynamics against which they had reacted. That development, in turn, spawned new reactions and calls for renewal within state church Protestantism in Britain and northern Europe. In this context, Puritanism and Pietism emerged. In many regards, these two streams have shaped the distinct theology and religious practice of contemporary evangelicalism in America more than the Reformation itself. Through Puritanism and Pietism, biblicism, crucicentrism, conversionism, and activism became dominant traits of the evangelical movement in colonial America.

Although the two strands had much in common, different emphases in theological language and religious practices of the various communities associated with Puritanism and Pietism emerged in the colonial era that endure within evangelicalism to this day. First, the two streams differed on the degree to which rigorous intellectual study of Scripture and powerful, personal, religious experience hold authority for faith and practice in the believing community. In oversimplified yet generally useful terms, Puritanism, especially in New England, put more emphasis on rigorous study as the primary source of religious authority, while Pietism stressed more the importance of a vital, personal, spiritual experience of the presence of God. Second, the two movements took a different approach to the relationship between religious and political authority for the sake of the common good. Puritans in New England saw the melding of political and religious authority as natural and necessary for social order, while Pietists in colonial America tended to hold political and religious authorities separate, believing that personal piety, more than political power, creates the foundation for social order in communities. However, we must be quick to add that individual churches and denominations within these two streams did not fully adhere to the general patterns described above.

Puritans were primitivists who sought to discipline their thoughts, emotions, and actions by their understanding of Scripture. For them, biblical truth was "first truth," that is, truth that had not been tainted and distorted by subsequent theologizing and institutionalization. As such, Puritans believed that the Bible narrated a time of pure faith and life. "It was the normative time to which the men and women of the present must, in imagination, 'return' for saving guidance and empowerment. And there they would find the crucial bearings for their own continuing venture through history."[11] For Puritans, the "speculations," theologizing, and religious practices of those who came after the first century did not hold the same authority as the biblical text, especially those theologies and practices too closely associated with Roman Catholicism. The goal of biblical study was to discern the meaning of the original texts and translate them, without perversion or embellishments from more than a millennium of Christian history, into contemporary life. Evangelicals use a very similar approach to hermeneutics and ecclesial practice today. It undergirds the emphasis on biblical studies in evangelical theological education.

Although Puritans in colonial America have been mocked as being excessively harsh, judgmental, prudish theocrats, their fundamental values and beliefs were driven far more by a vision for the common good than by the thirst for power and control. Their preaching focused on the complete efficacy of the death of Christ to accomplish redemption (crucicentrism) and transform individual lives (conversionism) and, through the godly lives of saved and transformed individuals, society itself (activism). The

31

Puritan influence in evangelical institutional approaches to theological education outweighs any other religious group from the colonial era. Through rigorous personal and intellectual discipline, Puritans in colonial America "achieved unprecedented levels of literacy, longevity and mass prosperity."[12]

Puritans established universities and institutions designed to bring order to a new civilization. They also expressed their conviction that church and state ought to work hand in hand to sustain that order through the establishment of state churches. "Establishments reflected the pervasive assumption that religion was so valuable in society that it deserved governmental support."[13] Some evangelicals in the colonies, however, believed that establishment inevitably leads to the spiritual malaise and corruption that the Reformers reacted against. Some Puritans reacted harshly to dissent while others granted latitude. Even in their earliest years in North America, evangelicals were divided over the question of how the church and the state ought to relate to one another. And we still can't seem to reach a consensus on the matter.

Pietism, although perhaps less discussed in American religious history than Puritanism, has shaped American evangelicalism more deeply and broadly than any other theological tradition. Sharing the Puritan convictions of biblicism and crucicentrism, albeit with its own emphases and formulations, Pietism brought conversionism and activism to the fore. As a reaction against the strict doctrinal conformity, dead formalism, and sacramentalism that came to characterize both Lutheran and Reformed churches in continental Europe, Pietists sought to create a deep personal experience and transformation on the Reformation foundations of *sola Scriptura, sola gratia, sola fide*, and *solus Christus*. "For all Pietists, this was the difference between merely nominal Christianity, the religion of mere 'professors of the faith,' and true Christianity. The former trusted in belief and ritual for salvation; the latter knew God experientially and transformatively in a personal and immediate way."[14] In many regards, Pietism created the primacy of a personal experience of God's presence and power unmediated by an ecclesial body or authority that becomes the hallmark of evangelicalism and permeates the movement today.

It would be a mistake to assume that Pietists undervalued theological orthodoxy and scriptural authority in their quest for more profound religious experience, although such an allegation has been leveled against more recent heirs of this tradition. Pietists took *sola Scriptura* very seriously and strongly emphasized biblical study. However, they approached the reading and study of the Bible in a way that diverged somewhat from the biblicism of the Puritans. They studied the Bible not just to understand it but to be transformed by the work of the Spirit through it. Pietists sought the inspiring and illuminating work of the Holy Spirit to guide their reading of Scripture. With their emphasis on the role of the Holy Spirit in helping a person understand the Bible, Pietists gave the Bible anew to the common man and made its reading and study the centerpiece of every believer's devotional life.

Unfortunately, in some evangelical denominations with roots in Pietism or at least sympathy with pietistic views of spirituality, this conviction has led to an undervaluing of formal theological education. I can remember preachers warning those of us who were "called to preach" against going to seminary because it would cause us to depend more upon "book learning" than upon the Spirit of God. And their warnings were justified to a certain degree. Traditional approaches to formal theological education have not valued religious experience as much as scholarship in curricular matters. Theological education for the next evangelicalism must value and incorporate both.

Pietism also established both social engagement and evangelism as essential parts of evangelical activism. Care for the poor and contribution to the good of society were characteristic values of early continental Pietists and other pietistic groups in America through the end of the nineteenth century. Pietism also played a significant role in the development of two key characteristics of the fledgling evangelicalism of England and North America in the eighteenth and nineteenth centuries: broadly ecumenical evangelistic outreach and the impulse to send missionaries around the globe to evangelize the lost in places where churches were not yet established. Both of these developments are hallmark characteristics of evangelicalism today and are foundational for understanding the most populous and dynamically growing streams within the movement: the Holiness and Pentecostal traditions, as well as charismatic renewal groups.

Although the theological heirs of Pietism have continued to stress the necessity and practice of ordered and intentional Bible study, it is their emphasis on powerful and personal spiritual experience that has become a hallmark of the way the majority of evangelicals in the United States approach their faith. Scriptural fidelity paired with powerful religious experience still defines evangelicalism. "If evangelical Christianity is anything, it is orthodoxy on fire, 'head belief' and 'heart experience' brought together. Evangelicals believe that these two dimensions—doctrine and devotion—belong together for holistic, authentic Christian life."[15]

Orthodoxy on fire. What a fitting turn of phrase for our movement. Dispassionate evangelicalism is as much an oxymoron as heretical evangelicalism. As a part of our fundamentalist legacy, we tend to focus our attention on shared convictions in defining evangelicalism, but shared religious experience is probably more universal than shared belief in our movement. Across denominational and doctrinal differences, evangelicals believe that we can relate to God personally, even intimately. We talk naturally and often about a "relationship with God," language those outside the movement find inscrutable but we find comforting and empowering. Theological education for the next evangelicalism must value and nurture this distinctive and formative feature of our movement.

5

Revive Us Again!

We had weeklong revival meetings twice a year at our local Baptist church. Nightly services with traveling evangelists serving up dire warnings of impending doom, passionate calls to repentance, and promises of eternal life were standard fare. From childhood I sat with the same church members singing the same hymns and listening to the same sermons and feeling guilty about the same sins twice a year, every year. And more than a few times I "went forward" to repent and be reassured that, because I had believed in Jesus, my sins were forgiven and the promise of heaven was still mine.

Evangelicalism is revivalist religion. It has been since the early eighteenth century and continues to be so today, albeit in more subtle and sophisticated forms. Through the Great Awakenings in the eighteenth and nineteenth centuries, the call for personal conversion (conversionism) through faith in the saving work of Jesus Christ on the cross (crucicentrism) became the hallmark of evangelicalism. Revivalist theology and ministry practices still shape our movement in the United States, including the way we do theological education. When we're willing to step away from what divides us, evangelicals find common ground in the belief that the gospel of Jesus Christ changes lives. This gospel gives us hope for the future. When that is our focus and identity, we are at our best.

As revivalist Christianity, evangelicalism assumes that conversion, spiritual formation, and mission can be experienced apart from the church. We begin to see the decoupling of soteriology and ecclesiology as early as the Reformation formulae—*sola gratia*, *sola fide*, *solus Christus*. The emphasis on personal transformation and spiritual formation in Pietism builds on that foundation. This decoupling of salvation and church, however, finds full voice in the great revivals of the eighteenth and nineteenth centuries. Some would argue that it is here, in the revivals of the Great Awakenings, that we evangelicals should seek our origins as a distinct movement within Protestantism that spans traditional theological and denominational lines. Put simply, in our revivalist roots we come to believe in and practice what could be experienced as essentially "churchless" Christianity. As one of my students recently put it, "Church is optional, you know?"

The Great Awakenings

Genuine revivals disrupt established religious structures and sensibilities, just as revolutions overturn established political structures and loyalties. Both are a form of rebellion. Some revivals bring about genuine change in established churches but have less impact in the broader society. Such was the case in some settings in Europe and the United Kingdom. In colonial America, however, the revival in the pews mingled with rebellion in the body politic. "In America the revivals transformed Protestantism. They undermined the established churches, led to the separation of church and state, and created a marketplace of religious ideas in which new sects and denominations flourished. At the same time, they made evangelical Protestantism the dominant force in the country for most of the nineteenth century."[1]

In some regards, the Great Awakenings showcased the competing values of rigorous theological reasoning and vigorous religious experience that characterized the exotic theological concoction of Puritanism and Pietism found in the Protestant presence in colonial America. Two luminaries of what is often called the First Great Awakening, Jonathan Edwards and George Whitefield, exemplify how these values created powerful and profound effects in the lives of those who heard them preach.[2] Edwards, whom many would see as the most significant theological mind in eighteenth-century America, was not known as an overly dramatic or emotional preacher. Rather, his sermons were dense theological and philosophical treatises. The power of his preaching lay in the theological depth and philosophical rigor of his messages. In his preaching Edwards emphasized themes woven throughout the fabric of Calvinism—human depravity, substitutionary atonement, justification by faith alone in Christ alone, and the glory of God. His preaching often created a powerful emotional response in many of his hearers. In Edwards one saw on full display the beautiful tension between reasoned intellectual inquiry and powerful emotional experience that would characterize evangelicalism for the next two centuries and beyond.

If Edwards was the theological and philosophical muse of the First Great Awakening, the cross-eyed, theatrically trained, itinerant preacher George Whitefield was its celebrity. An Englishman by birth, innkeeper by occupation, Calvinist by conviction, and evangelist by calling, Whitefield was the most widely known preacher in the English-speaking world. Preaching mostly extemporaneously, he drew thousands of people from all walks of life to his sermons and commanded their attention like no other speaker they had ever heard. Sarah Edwards described the impact of Whitefield's preaching on those who came to listen. "It is wonderful to see what a spell he cast over an audience by proclaiming the simplest truths of the Bible. I have seen upwards of a thousand people hang on his words with breathless silence, broken only by an occasional half-suppressed sob. He impresses the ignorant, and not less the educated and refined. . . . He speaks from a heart all aglow with love, and pours out a torrent of eloquence which is almost irresistible."[3]

Whitefield's influence on evangelicalism in the colonies greatly exceeded what he accomplished in Britain. He was the "first inter-colonial celebrity" whose every move was chronicled and every sermon, seemingly, disseminated by the print media of the day. After just one year of Whitefield's itinerating through the colonies and preaching to crowds greater than any speaker had ever addressed in America, "evangelicalism had turned into a countrywide movement with a radical wing fomenting religious rebellion."[4] It is not too much of a stretch to see the First Great Awakening as the beginning of evangelicalism's ascendancy in the religious life of populist America. From New England through the middle colonies and into the South, revivalist evangelical expressions of religious faith shook established religious institutions to the core and put them on notice that religion in America would organize and express itself very differently than British and continental Protestantism.

The revivals of the early to mid-eighteenth century established several features of evangelicalism that endure to this day: the deinstitutionalization of salvation and personal spiritual renewal; the prevalence and effectiveness of cross-denominational evangelism and mission efforts; the willingness to adopt new technologies, structures, and methods to advance the preaching of the gospel; and the emergence of the preacher as celebrity.

The Great Awakening tilled the fertile soil of dissatisfaction within the rigid and socially stratified society that Puritanism had helped create in New England. It also provided emotional energy and theological justification to the impetus toward disestablishment. The revivals gave common people—those with no clerical authority, formal education, or theological training—a voice and a platform from which to exhort others to repentance and a vital faith in Jesus Christ. "A new era of spiritual democracy had begun."[5] Personal testimonies of conversion took religious truth out of the hands of clergy and placed it in the hearts and voices of the laity, regardless of their social status, wealth, education, and vocation. Throughout our history evangelicals have turned to personal testimonies of spiritual transformation to validate and energize our own faith commitments. The passionate voices of common people narrating powerful and transformative encounters with God often made the reasoned arguments of formally trained theologians sound cold and irrelevant. Outside of New England, clergy trained in theological colleges and seminaries often found themselves with much to say but few who would listen.

Laypeople, however, who had experienced a profound transformative work of God in their lives, found themselves with many who would listen but had not much more to say than their own personal testimony of faith. Evangelicalism as populist religion finds its footing in this era.[6]

The Great Awakening also aroused passionate opposition to the established churches of colonial England and, in turn, significant persecution from those very churches. In some cases, revivalist preachers were jailed for "disturbing the peace." Disestablishment of any state church, a hallmark of the political philosophy that would come to dominate the attitude of the nation, brought evangelicals, more theologically liberal Christians, Deists, and Unitarians together. "The evangelicals wanted disestablishment so they could freely preach the gospel; the rationalists and deists wanted disestablishment because they felt an enlightened government should not punish people for their religious views. The combination of the two would transform America, helping make it both intensely religious and religiously free."[7]

When war broke out between the colonists in America and the British Crown, many evangelicals believed it to be a religious war that portended the apocalypse through which the "righteous" would establish the kingdom of God by defeating the enemies of God. At the head of this list of enemies were the British monarchy, which many asserted had descended into moral bankruptcy with its oppressive politics and greed, and French Roman Catholics, who were threatening to take for themselves territory that God had given to the Protestant colonialists. To the revolutionaries, God, it seemed, was bringing a new nation into existence for his special purpose, or, at least, he was providentially guiding the actions of those who would birth it. "During and after the Revolution, many people conflated America's political affairs with divine purposes, which lent an aura of redemptiveness to the war and to the agenda of a fledgling nation."[8] This wouldn't be the last war that Americans would wage as a God-ordained campaign.

The temptation to conflate "America's political affairs with divine purposes" has bedeviled evangelicalism since the First Great

Awakening. Disestablishment, revivalist religion, and conversionist piety lay no foundation upon which evangelicals can create a cohesive view of the dual identity of believer and citizen. Our revivalist conversionism and impoverished ecclesiology, with no clear mandate for living out one's kingdom identity, have provided the loam from which Christian nationalism has flourished among evangelicals. In like manner, our biblicism without the critical structures of moral and political philosophy baptizes and scandalizes in equal measure individual nations, governments, politicians, and policies, depending upon an evangelical's sense of which ones would lead to the free exercise of faith and the pursuit of personal prosperity. It's clear that evangelicalism has yet to craft a coherent public theology that embodies our gospel hope, justice demands, and compassion mandate. In fact, the lack of such continues to erode our credibility in the broader society today.

Theological education in the colonial era took two distinct forms. On the one hand, the early institutions of higher education in the colonies—Harvard, William and Mary, and Yale—were all founded by religious groups and had distinctly theological curricula and goals. Adopting the basic model of an English or Scottish university, these schools sought to educate white men who would serve the church and the civil state. A second form of theological education emerged in the expansion of both geographical and spiritual frontiers. Moving far beyond the practical reach of established institutions, evangelists and ministers had no opportunity for formal theological instruction. Some simply saw no value in it. Their gospel work, laced with the urgency of offering salvation to as many as possible, provided no impetus to deeper reflection and rigorous study. Many of them apprenticed with established ministers; some used denominational resources to enhance their knowledge of Scripture. Most simply studied the Bible fervently on their own in order to prepare their next sermon. Many Black preachers mentored younger men and women in the theology, spirituality, and practices of their congregations. Often denied access to formal education, these preachers created a legacy of powerfully formative, life-based theological education that has served Black churches for generations. Throughout our history the number of pastors and evangelists engaged in informal, practice-based theological training has far outpaced the number of those seeking formal university-level training in theological colleges and seminaries. The same is true today.

In spite of its broad popularity, the influence of evangelical expressions of Protestantism diminished among the educational and political elites in the colonies after the tumult of the American Revolution. The disruption of the war itself added to that decline. By the time the foundational documents of the new nation were drafted, the most influential voices—Washington, Jefferson, Madison, Hamilton, and others—came from those whose views were more secular, unitarian, and deistic.

The waning influence of evangelicals in the formation of the nation's founding documents, however, did not represent a diminishing of the populist demand for the life promised by the dozens of itinerant revival preachers who coursed through the expanding territory of the young nation. The adaptive nature of evangelical thought and methods, along with the compelling hope of a better life that revivalist gospel proclamation promised, led to a renewed populist presence and influence of evangelicals as America entered the nineteenth century. Its preaching and practice resonated with the cry of the Baptist, Methodist, and African American churches for freedom, as well as the plea for social order, commonsense morality, and rationalism that the more established churches voiced. White evangelicals found themselves in both populist and establishmentarian camps. Although some groups disagreed theologically on some matters and distrusted each other politically, they created "a social juggernaut" that became the most influential religious presence in America.

Although it may have been absent in the founding documents of the nation, evangelical thought and practice provided much of the glue that held together an expanding but already fracturing nation. Culturally, the evangelical message of personal salvation and renewal resonated with the optimism of the new nation and the individualism of a population expanding westward, far away from the established educational institutions, intellectual elites, and seats of government in New England and the Middle Atlantic states. Perhaps even more importantly, however, white evangelicals promoted "the belief that the United States was a chosen land designated by God for special, even millennial, purposes." In so doing, they denied the reality of the experience of enslaved Africans and their descendants, many of whom professed and preached the same gospel, while they "enhanced their own position as the definers of the meaning of America."[9] This temptation continues to woo our movement into the idolatrous worship of an idealized caricature of our nation and its history. "Who gets to define America?" has been a powerful battle cry of the culture wars. We cannot hope to address those values and beliefs that have contributed to our current crisis of identity and mission unless we are willing to honestly tell the story of the movement's place in the history of the nation, including its role in the establishment and perpetuation of race-based slavery in "God's chosen nation."

Between the Revolutionary War and the end of the nineteenth century, another series of powerful revivals (often dubbed the Second and Third Great Awakenings) further established evangelicalism as the most prominent religious presence in the United States. During the first half of the nineteenth century, evangelicals, especially in the emerging territories and states of the American interior, established many of the social services and cultural institutions, including schools, hospitals, churches, and publishing houses, upon which the growing population depended for survival and social order. Although united in addressing many of the nation's needs through evangelistic preaching and social reform efforts, evangelicals could not come to a consensus on the nation's most pernicious national sins—white supremacy, racism, and institutionalized race-based slavery. That failure reflected the deeper divides—culturally, economically, and educationally—that would eventually lead to war.

Evangelicalism and the Civil War

Mark Noll's notable work *The Civil War as a Theological Crisis* demonstrates how nineteenth-century evangelicalism's biblicism and theology not only failed to avert the Civil War but likely contributed to its inevitability.[10] Within white evangelicalism, both able defenders of slavery and abolitionists claimed biblical support for their antithetical positions. And both sides could be found in the North and in the South. The hermeneutical schism was not based purely on regional differences, although abolitionists were rarer in the South than defenders of slavery were in the North. The cost of that schism staggers the mind. The "children of the Revival"[11] took up arms against one another, both sides convinced that theirs was a holy cause because it was undergirded by God's Word. Evangelicalism's broad reach of inclusion across theological, denominational, regional, educational, and economic divisions magnified the catastrophic failure of its preachers and theologians to come to a point of agreement on whether the Bible sanctioned or prohibited slavery. Our theology and hermeneutics simply failed to change the deep assumptions and values that undergirded the dehumanization, enslavement, and abuse of trafficked Africans.

Before the war, the Bible occupied a lofty place in the new nation. Broadly distributed and regularly read in homes, schools, and churches, the Bible came to be seen as the source of answers for any and all of life's questions. Once the Bible was elevated at the expense of theological tradition and ecclesial institutions, its authority lay in the interpretations of individual preachers and readers. Its meaning was assumed to be "plain" and its application to life "clear." The Bible rendered the world "understandable" and "simple." Biblicism leaves little middle ground for common cause between those who read a text differently. The potent blend of Enlightenment certainty and biblicism, a formula that had grounded American optimism and industry in the formation of the new republic while at the same time providing theological cover for race-based slavery in the South, now poisoned the hermeneutical controversy over slavery with a fanaticism that made compromise impossible. The assumptions evangelicals held about the Bible and its interpretation "transformed the conclusions reached by opponents into willful perversions of sacred truth and natural reason."[12] Broad disregard for, if not disparagement of, intellectually and theologically rigorous theological education in populist, revivalist religion creates no foundation for resolving differences of interpretation on matters with significant import in the lives of the faithful. Many parts of our movement still struggle with a "winner take all" approach to biblical hermeneutics when confronted with opposing interpretations of passages.

In the hermeneutical debates over slavery leading up to the war, its defenders had the upper hand. In both the Old and New Testaments, one could find verses that described, sanctioned, and regulated slavery. Those who argued against this "clear" teaching of Scripture were accused of denying the plain meaning of the texts and undermining the authority of God's Word. Proponents of abolition, on the other hand, typically used more-nuanced arguments that depended upon theological assumptions, a consideration of the original contexts of the passages in question, and an appeal to universal morality. This approach was too complex for most Bible readers and preachers. It challenged the now sacred belief that anyone could pick up the Bible, read it, see its plain meaning, and march into the complexities of the day with a simple answer for all of life's questions.

The early leaders in the Southern Baptist Convention (SBC), whose founding in 1845 was associated with the advocacy of slavery as an institution endorsed by the Bible and permitted by God's providence, used both hermeneutical and theological arguments to justify the dehumanizing enslavement of trafficked Africans. Hermeneutically the approach was summarized by Richard Fuller, one of the largest slaveholders in South Carolina and president of the SBC from 1859 to 1863. Concerning slavery, he said, "What God sanctioned in the Old Testament and permitted in the New Testament cannot be sin."[13] Although some disagreed with this approach, most Baptist pastors in the South had no formal theological training in a seminary or college and could offer little to refute Fuller's argument. In fact, many leaders in the denomination either opposed, or diminished the importance of, formal theological education for pastors.

As if the inability of evangelicals to find in their hermeneutics and theology a way forward to avert war wasn't devastating enough, another tragic oversight in their debates over slavery would have even longer-lasting consequences. Both sides failed to address adequately the underlying assumption of white superiority upon which race-based slavery was built. Both abolitionists and defenders of slavery failed to critique the essential dehumanization of people of African descent that undergirded an economy built on the commodification of human beings. Noll writes, "So seriously fixed in the minds of white Americans, including most abolitionists, was the certainty of black racial inferiority that it overwhelmed biblical testimony about race, even though most Protestant Americans claimed that Scripture was in fact their supreme authority in adjudicating such matters."[14] This oversight determined that the defeat of the South in the Civil War, the Emancipation Proclamation, and the Constitutional amendments that followed did not change the deeply entrenched racist assumptions that many white evangelicals, including ardent abolitionists, accepted uncritically or, at best, resignedly.

Some white evangelicals openly participated in the Ku Klux Klan's acts of intimidation and violence and in the public lynchings of black people, while some spoke out and actively worked to oppose the sustained and codified racial injustice of the Jim Crow era. Most, however, remained silent. Jemar Tisby describes the effects of that silence.

> Many white Christians failed to unequivocally condemn lynching and other acts of racial terror. Doing so poisoned the American legal system and made Christian churches complicit in racism for generations. While some Christians spoke out and denounced

these lynchings (just as some Christians called for abolition), the majority stance of the American church was avoidance, turning a blind eye to the practice. It's not that members of every white church participated in lynching, but the practice could not have endured without the relative silence, if not outright support, of one of the most significant institutions in America, the Christian church.[15]

The complicity of white evangelicals in propogating the malignant and pernicious presence of racism in the United States remains our deepest shame. It must not be ignored, explained away, or soothed. It must be faced with clear-eyed honesty. Theological education for the next evangelicalism must lead the movement to do so.

The failure to address deeply rooted notions of white supremacy guaranteed that racism would continue to plague our movement and the nation for generations to come. Although white evangelicals embarked on a grand expansion of gospel proclamation nationally and internationally in the late nineteenth and early twentieth century, churches, revivals, and seminaries remained segregated in the United States. Evangelical missionaries would cross the ocean to preach to Africans, but some of them would not share a pew with the sons and daughters of emancipated African slaves in their homeland. Widely acclaimed preachers like Dwight L. Moody, Billy Sunday, and Charles G. Finney allowed segregated seating at their revivals. When Frederick Douglass compared Moody's Philadelphia campaign with the public lecture there of noted agnostic Robert Ingersoll, he said, "The negro can go into the circus, the theatre, and can be admitted to the lectures of Mr. Ingersoll, but he cannot go into an evangelical Christian meeting."[16]

As the nation nursed its war wounds and continued to expand its territory, the revivals went on in both black and white churches. Once again, they established evangelicalism as a relatively distinct movement within Protestantism and carried it into the twentieth century as the most widely embraced expression of Christianity in America. But it wasn't just through revivals that evangelicals made their presence known. Many worked tirelessly to address the physical, social, and spiritual needs of those who were victimized by alcoholism, family violence, and unfair labor practices: women, children, and the poor. They "organized myriad voluntary societies and poured their energies into the causes of hospitals, schools, orphanages, prison reform, temperance laws, peace activism, recreation and leisure organizations, Sunday education for working children, the outlawing of dueling, services to native Americans and the poor, and the reform of prostitutes, drunks, and other dishonorable elements of any Christian civilization."[17] Black churches provided sanctuary from the stifling oppression and deprivation of the Jim Crow era. In many cases they created the social structures, services, and advocacy that legally sanctioned and culturally accepted segregation denied black Americans. In almost every regard black churches developed and expressed a much more robust and meaningful ecclesiology than most white churches, an ecclesiology that sought transformation in both the individual and the community.[18]

Changing immigration patterns and urbanization created a new challenge and evangelistic opportunity for evangelicals in the latter years of the nineteenth century. It also helped spawn a new kind of theological school, one more adapted to missionary work and the educational backgrounds and aspirations of those who sensed God's call to it. Falling somewhere between the formal university model of established denominational seminaries and the less formal mentoring programs of preachers in churches on the frontier, Bible colleges emerged as a new kind of theological education designed "to get Christian workers to the urban mission field as soon as possible with the practical, how-to knowledge needed to do that work."[19] Bible colleges, some of which became accredited seminaries or spawned such, have trained more people for ministry, by far, than accredited, graduate-level evangelical seminaries.

Evangelicalism's influence spread far beyond the boundaries of the United States. The conviction that salvation can be found only through belief in the gospel of Jesus Christ drove us to engage in an ambitious mobilization of the church to take that message around the globe. American evangelical missionaries were sent to Africa, Latin America, and Asia. They went with zeal, conviction, and a willingness to sacrifice their own lives so that all could hear the gospel. The evangelical missionary movement of the nineteenth century laid the foundation for an ongoing commitment to fulfill Christ's command "to make disciples of all nations" that largely defined evangelicalism through the first three quarters of the twentieth century. The expansion of evangelical theology and practice around the globe remains one of the most remarkable mobilizations of the church in history.

To be sure, evangelicalism has never been a cohesive movement. It certainly wasn't in the latter half of the nineteenth century. Its theological DNA—biblicism, crucicentrism, conversionism, and activism—accommodates striking diversity denominationally, politically, sociologically, economically, regionally, ethnically, and racially (while remaining largely segregated). Even with this diversity, the movement has retained a distinct presence and identity in the broader landscape of American religious affiliation. Simply put, evangelicalism was the single most influential religious presence in American society for most of the nineteenth century, and its success strengthened the pervasive belief among white evangelicals that the United States was favored by God to become the embodiment of his kingdom. That optimism, however, would soon be shaken.

6

The Quest for Credibility

The evangelicalism that became the most influential and widely respected religious movement in the nation waned in the latter years of the nineteenth century and essentially disappeared in the first three decades of the twentieth century, fracturing into liberal and fundamentalist camps. As in any messy divorce, both sides displayed more animus than Christian charity toward one another. That divorce and its aftermath set the framework for the emergence of evangelicalism, sometimes dubbed "neo-evangelicalism" by fundamentalists, as we know it today.

Although few of us are comfortable admitting it, we are the heirs of fundamentalism. Our theology, values, and practices still bear traits and tendencies of that heritage. Coming to terms with its lingering presence remains a pressing concern for our movement. Just as the evangelicalism we experience today emerged as a reaction to fundamentalism, the next evangelicalism must carve out an identity even further removed from the values, hermeneutics, and social posture of our fundamentalist heritage and those who find comfort in it. Nothing less than the identity and credibility of our movement are at stake in the pursuit of this vision.

Fundamentalism

To sustain momentum and energize the faithful, renewal movements need new threats and enemies to react against. The instinct to preserve the movement's beliefs, values, and practices against enemies, both perceived and real, strengthens the resolve of the faithful to defend its boundaries and sustain its unique identity. The possibility of threat from contrarian ideas or practices taking root inside the movement provides justification for authoritarian leadership to take punitive action against those who are suspected of entertaining such deviance. Christian fundamentalism does not differ from other religious fundamentalist movements in this regard. And, to be frank, it does not differ from the social dynamic of liberal orthodoxy either.

Two perceived threats to evangelical convictions and the viability of the movement loomed large at the end of the nineteenth century—naturalism and modernism. Naturalism, the belief that all reality can only be understood through natural causes, denied the possibility of the supernatural in the physical realm. It challenged evangelical convictions about the truthfulness of the Bible, God's act of creation, his immanence, and his providence, including his intervention in human experience through miracles. Modernism, postulating an optimism that humans can continually improve themselves and their environments through the development and adoption of new ideas, technologies, and structures, threatened the essentially primitivist instincts of a movement that held fast to a set of beliefs established centuries before and the conviction that a simple reading of the Bible held the answer to all of life's questions no matter what other sources of knowledge may aver. Although evangelicals were quick to adopt new methods and technologies for the sake of mission, they remained skeptical about new developments or approaches in theological understanding and biblical hermeneutics, particularly those that seemed to pose a threat to biblical inerrancy. Anything "new" when applied to theology and hermeneutics challenges the fundamentalist myth that we have already recovered biblical truth, rescuing it from the distortions of Roman Catholicism, and are now living out the pure faith of the New Testament. In addition, an optimistic view of humanity's ability to improve the world collided with the growing popularity of a dispensational apocalypticism that saw the future trajectory of human history through the lens of decline and doom. With a surge of immigrants from historically Roman Catholic countries into America's major cities, evangelicals sensed they were losing their place in society as the definer of American identity, values, and religious faith. And they were.

What made these intellectual and social developments even more threatening was their adoption by leaders in denominations and schools that evangelicals had considered their own. It was one thing for the broader culture and public universities to adopt naturalistic assumptions like those postulated by Darwinism, but when preachers and professors in historically evangelical institutions began to question the supernatural character and historical reliability of the biblical record with those same assumptions, the threat demanded a reaction. Since we tend to view theology as a bounded set of self-evident truths that are meant to be passed down from one generation to the next, when we sense those truths are threatened, our natural response is to circle the wagons around a required reaffirmation of them, reject arguments that question them, and vigorously defend our ideological boundaries by attacking those who challenge them.

And that's just what the most conservative groups within evangelicalism did. In the second decade of the twentieth century, several pastors and professors published twelve volumes of essays entitled *The Fundamentals: A Testimony to the Truth*.[1] Three million copies were mailed to almost exclusively white pastors, professors, and missionaries. The essays "opposed all kinds of modernism, from biblical higher criticism to theological liberalism, from naturalism to Darwinism to democratic socialism."[2] It is doubtful that any other treatise on theology and hermeneutics ever matched the distribution of *The Fundamentals*. Although it may be too simplistic to say that the publication of these essays marked the beginning of the fundamentalist movement, it would not be an overstatement to affirm that the essays became the consensus baseline for theological and ecclesiastical affinity in fundamentalism. The impulse continually to reaffirm the theological foundations of a movement in order to fortify its ideological boundaries and reinforce the commitment of the faithful remains a powerful value in some streams of our movement today.

Up to this point, evangelicalism had somehow managed to embrace a strikingly diverse menagerie of denominations, theologians, preachers, churches, and other ministry organizations. But in the first half of the twentieth century, the tone of the movement's engagement with the broader culture and the tenor of the internal conversation among fellow evangelicals changed. The "children of the revival" waged war with one another again, this time with verbal barrages aimed to secure the hearts of the already faithful, shame dissenters back into the fold, and pronounce judgment on the "unbelievers." Denominations, mission agencies, local churches, friends, and families found themselves at odds with those with whom they had once been united. Not even the mission impulse to preach the gospel to all nations could overcome the divisions between those who pledged allegiance to *The Fundamentals* and those who in good conscience could not affirm some of the document's contents or would not adopt the pugilistic tone of those who weaponized it.

Although significant differences in religious thought and practice between the ranks of evangelicals who were educated in elite universities and the populist throngs in the pews of most evangelical churches had always existed, both sides were now forced to make a choice. The predominantly white religious movement we have been calling evangelicalism up to this point essentially disappeared into competing identities of fundamentalist and "mainline" (read "liberal") Protestantism. Two watershed issues drove the divide: the Bible and the gospel, the former believed by fundamentalists to be the only foundation upon which one could affirm the latter.

Regarding the Bible, fundamentalists opposed any form of interpretive method that raised questions about, or could possibly imply any doubt about, the truthfulness of the biblical text. They rejected the possibility that it contained errors of any kind, even though it had been written by human authors whose knowledge was limited by their humanity and their historical context. Fundamentalists affirmed that the Bible could not contain errors of any sort because it was inspired by a God who has perfect knowledge of all things. They defended the plenary verbal inspiration and authority of the biblical text in all matters. Any knowledge or conclusion that contradicted the clear teaching of the Bible when read in its "plain" sense must be deemed false, regardless of the evidence that could be marshaled to support it.

Battles over the nature of the Bible and how to interpret it roiled established Protestant theological schools. Daniel O. Aleshire describes how three different schools handled the controversy. "Southern Baptist Theological Seminary, Union Theological Seminary in New York, and Princeton Theological Seminary all had major controversies over faculty who were using new scholarly methods to teach the Bible. What differed was how each resolved it: Southern dismissed a faculty member who used modern scholarly methods in the 1870s; Union severed its Presbyterian connections rather than dismiss an accused professor in the 1890s; and some conservative faculty members at Princeton, having lost control of the faculty, left to start a new seminary in the 1920s."[3] Many evangelical seminaries today find their origins in this kind of controversy. An abiding tension in evangelical theological education revolves around the application of critical methods to the study of Scripture. An abiding fear for most of these schools is that they will be accused of "liberalism" in their approach to the Bible, an accusation that will alienate constituents and drive away donors en masse.

Regarding the nature of the gospel, in spite of the historic engagement of evangelicals in meeting the social needs of an expanding nation, some fundamentalists feared that the so-called social gospel[4] substituted social work for evangelism, the feeding of bodies for the saving of souls. In many places, fundamentalists continued the care for the poor that had characterized evangelicalism in the nineteenth century, with their ultimate goal the salvation of individual souls more than the end of the systemic injustice that perpetuated such dire social needs. Just as they had evangelized enslaved Africans before and during the war without directly addressing the underlying white supremacy and racism upon which chattel slavery thrived, fundamentalists reaffirmed their conviction that gospel proclamation must always trump social engagement.[5] It was one thing for evangelicals to argue over the interpretation of the Bible and its application to life, but when they could not agree on the nature of the gospel itself, the fracturing of evangelicalism became inevitable. Unfortunately, the two questions that led to the splintering of evangelicalism into fundamentalist and liberal camps—the nature of biblical revelation and the nature of the gospel—remain flash points of conflict for some in our movement today.

Many fundamentalists also adopted premillennial dispensationalism as a framework for reading biblical prophecy, interpreting current affairs, and creating a vision of the "end times." Popularized through the *Scofield Reference Bible* and widely attended Bible conferences, and institutionalized through Moody Bible Institute and Dallas Theological Seminary, this biblical and cultural hermeneutic provided a seemingly clear framework for understanding God's engagement in human history in the past and the future. It spawned an almost single-minded preoccupation with the timing and events associated with the second coming of Christ. Gospel proclamation was couched in the framework of escape from certain doom when Christ comes to judge those who have not been saved. Further, the truly saved would be rescued from the prophesied horrors of this world through the rapture of the saints. An escapist soteriology and eschatology left little reason to engage the social needs of this world. If the world would soon be destroyed, why should the faithful waste their efforts trying to improve it?[6]

Fundamentalist rhetoric introduced a powerful and enduring meme in evangelicalism that would later be coined "the slippery slope." Fundamentalists warn against the danger of new ideas or innovations because one small deviation from an accepted truth or required practice of the group would inevitably lead to further deviation and, eventually, the abandonment of the whole. Phrases such as "creeping liberalism" capture this threat well and ratchet up the fear of an unknown maleficent presence in one's own community that will ultimately lead others into apostasy. This meme remains very powerful in evangelicalism, especially when used to describe seminaries and Christian colleges. Some donors will not give to permanently endowed funds because they fear a school may follow the example of some evangelically postured seminaries that eventually adopted liberal theological and ethical views.

Within fundamentalism, the belief that one deviation inevitably leads to the abandonment of the whole remains a pervasive line of argument in defense of biblical inerrancy. Thus, if one questions whether God created all things in six literal twenty-four-hour days as described in Genesis 1-2, the inevitable outcome, fundamentalists warn, will be rejection of the historical accuracy of the Gospels' accounts of the life, death, and resurrection of Jesus Christ. Fear of denying the whole because one part of it is questioned creates a powerful deterrent to innovative thinking and an unassailable platform of religious authority for those who make it their solemn duty to maintain the ideological purity and behavioral boundaries of the movement. Evangelical theological schools live in the constant tension of pushing back the boundaries of knowledge while holding fast to and regularly reaffirming their allegiance to the core convictions of the movement, all the while looking over their right shoulders to make sure they haven't gone far enough to draw the ire of the boundary keepers.

While fundamentalists turned their verbal guns on one another and marched toward division, the broader culture ran apace after the intellectual freedom and social optimism naïvely promised by naturalism, scientism, and modernism. Whatever voice evangelicals may have had in the intellectual climate of the country at the close of the nineteenth century disappeared in the first three decades of the twentieth. The Scopes trial (1925) epitomizes the demise of evangelical influence. As a result of the negative publicity generated by the trial, "fundamentalism came to be viewed as out of date and obscurantist. By 1930 it was clear that America had rejected the fundamentalist version of a restored Christian civilization,"[7] and the movement embraced its new, self-acclaimed identity as a persecuted minority. Withdrawal from public discourse did not, however, mean cessation of hostilities. Fundamentalist rhetoric condemning those who did not agree wholeheartedly with its tenets and its separatist posture continued to scorch the faithful and the infidel alike.

While retreat from broader cultural engagement in the face of searing scorn from national media outlets and public intellectuals would portend defeat for most social entities, such was not the case with fundamentalism. Fundamentalist churches and schools, battered and bruised from within and without, continued to grow throughout the middle years of the twentieth century. Although theological liberals had taken control of the country's oldest and most academically respected colleges and seminaries and placed leaders sympathetic to their theological perspective in the largest historical Protestant denominations, the identity of a "mocked and scorned martyr for the faith" energized fundamentalist leaders and increased group loyalty among the faithful. This identity and rhetoric of a persecuted and aggrieved minority remain quite persuasive in our movement, especially around the issue of religious freedom.[8] They also make us easy prey for fearmongering preachers, pundits, and politicians.

Although many of the staunch fundamentalist institutions and churches that took the lead in defining the movement were in the South, it would be a mistake to assume that fundamentalism was just a regional phenomenon. Many of the public figures in fundamentalism were from northern states and Southern California.[9] It would also be erroneous to assume that fundamentalism only appealed to the working class. Its dominant values of theological, hermeneutical, and moral certainty and its clear identity markers, separation, conservatism, authoritarian leadership, and intolerance of deviation or disloyalty appealed to a broad cross section of the American population. For many, fundamentalist beliefs, values, and behaviors create a sense of intellectual and ethical security in a world that feels increasingly complex and threatening.

Fundamentalists created their own educational institutions and, depending on the degree of separation from "secularists and liberals" they practiced, did battle with the broader Christian community and secular society on their own terms. They didn't really care what the world thought about them because they didn't think much of the world. In the 1930s and '40s their churches and schools grew robustly throughout the heartland. Frances FitzGerald describes how fundamentalist leaders used the perceived, and sometimes real, scorn of outsiders to strengthen the commitment of their followers. "On the whole, cultural exile suited the fundamentalist leaders. Indeed, some stepped deliberately into outsider roles, portraying themselves as martyrs and the faithful as a beleaguered remnant fighting the Devil incarnate in all the forces of the secular and the apostate world. This stance inspired conspiracy theories of the vilest sort, but also fostered group solidarity and attracted Bible-believing Protestants alienated in the strange new world of global depression and global war. From their wanderings in the wilderness, the fundamentalists emerged stronger than before."[10] The identity, mentality, and emotional posture of an embattled minority continue to play a very strong role in evangelicalism today. They form a narrative by which one interprets reality, speculates about the future, and navigates the news, popular media, politics, even life in the church. Donald Trump expertly exploited this aggrieved and embattled minority narrative to lure evangelicals into believing that he was on their side. And millions of evangelicals, willingly ignoring his narcissism, pathological mendacity, and moral vacuity, took the bait.

Fundamentalist leaders maintained that the boundaries of orthodoxy must be clearly drawn and everyone has to declare whether they are "in" or "out." Powerful preachers and evangelists whipped up the faithful by decrying modernists and secularists and promising certain destruction for those who dare abide their ideas or even enjoy their company. Not surprisingly, fundamentalist leaders often attacked one another, questioning whether someone truly holds to the fundamentals of the faith if that person's teaching seems to diverge, even in the smallest detail or nuance, from the plain reading of Scripture and the "faith once delivered." Fundamentalism must control its theological and behavioral boundaries in order to retain its integrity. Public shame, ostracism, and fear-mongering are frequently used to reinforce those boundaries and build loyalty to the leaders who patrol them. With no overarching ecclesiastical authority to referee the fracas, preachers and ministry leaders take upon themselves a religious authority that is ripe for abuse. The specter of a pope in every pulpit is closer to reality than most evangelicals care to admit.

While the theological and hermeneutical controversies that led to the formation of fundamentalism as a separate religious identity raged in the cities and the national press, a powerful movement within evangelicalism continued to sweep the countryside. Driven by a desire to pursue holy living, passionate worship, and a powerful experience of the abiding presence of the Holy Spirit in their lives, denominations whose theological roots were found primarily in Pietism and Methodism experienced unprecedented growth in the late nineteenth and early twentieth century. This growth multiplied in the Holiness, Pentecostal, and charismatic movements among both white and black churches. These groups shared a "yearning simply to know the divine mind and will as directly and as purely as possible, without the distorting refractions of human volition, traditions, and speculations."[11] Whereas the public disputes between fundamentalists, liberals, and moderate evangelicals were waged almost exclusively by white men, leadership in the Holiness, Pentecostal, and charismatic movements was often racially mixed and gender inclusive.

Although denominations associated with these movements make up the single largest bloc of evangelicals in the world today, their place in evangelical theological and historical scholarship has been underexplored and undervalued. On the one hand, the movements' emphasis on religious experience over "cold rationalism" seems to diminish the value they place on theological education and scholarship. But on the other hand, many evangelical theological schools simply don't know how to incorporate Pentecostal and charismatic epistemology and practice into their pursuit of academic respectability. Some dispensational schools teach that charismatic gifts and phenomena—speaking in tongues, prophetic pronouncements, miraculous healing—ceased with the close of the New Testament canon. The critical issue for these schools is the nature of revelation—how God makes himself known and how we may know him. Many evangelical seminaries and their faculty members, even those who do not adopt a cessationist view, simply undervalue the importance of religious experience in theological method and knowledge, especially experience that is particularly emotive and expressive.[12] Since most evangelical seminaries are predominately white institutions, the more expressive, interactive, and testimony-based epistemologies, theologies, and religious experience of black and Hispanic churches have less presence and credence in our scholarship and worship. As a result, many denominations associated with Pentecostalism and charismatic renewal did not, and still do not, recommend formal theological education in accredited seminaries for their ministers.

The fundamentalist rejection and liberalism's accommodation of naturalism and modernism in hermeneutics and theology forced evangelicals to take sides and made it ever more difficult to find middle ground between the two warring factions of Protestantism. Some evangelicals wanted to hold fast to the inspiration, inerrancy, and authority of Scripture while adopting critical and scientific approaches to its study. Many liberal theologians held that the assumptions of biblicism precluded an honest scholarly approach to hermeneutics and theology. Further, some evangelicals believed that the biblical gospel demanded both a call for repentance of individual sins and engagement in the dismantling of systemic injustice. Fundamentalists felt that social engagement was an abandonment of the gospel; many liberals believed that a gospel of individual salvation was incomplete. Liberals and fundamentalists hardened their positions and took no prisoners in denouncing and heaping scorn on one another.

Through it all, the credibility and social respect that evangelicalism had earned in the nineteenth century waned. What had been a credible and compelling religious movement that shaped American thought and values on a national level became an isolated sectarian cultural outcast in the eyes and voices of those shaping the national conversation on religion, science, ethics, and government. Fundamentalists and liberal Protestants fed one another's pathetically unnuanced and mean-spirited stereotypes. It's no wonder that a cultural and religious no-man's-land developed between the battle lines.

Some evangelicals, however, desired to engage the intellectual climate and social needs of the day from the foundation of historical evangelical theological commitments. They set out to understand and articulate their faith in conversation with the intellectual challenges of naturalism, scientism, and modernism while remaining engaged in professions and institutions that were shaping American culture. Most of all they lamented the damage to the credibility of the gospel and the loss of evangelicalism's place at the table of American intellectual life. Unfortunately, their voices were drowned out by the anger and vitriol of both fundamentalists and secularists. They would not be heard until the 1940s.

Neo-Evangelicalism

Evangelicals with conservative instincts, who held to the essential doctrines exposited in *The Fundamentals* but lamented the militant tone, separatist tendencies, and cultural disengagement of the more strident fundamentalists, sought to stay involved in the intellectual, political, social, and cultural affairs of the nation. Their goal was to rebuild a credible and winsome gospel presence. They wanted to address the stereotypes in the national press and in the broader culture that evangelicals were "anti-intellectual" and unconcerned about social needs. The

National Association of Evangelicals (NAE), with a seven-point doctrinal statement that reflected the core theological tenets of *The Fundamentals*, came onto the national scene in 1943. The energy around its creation spawned lobbying organizations (Office of Public Affairs and the National Religious Broadcasters), professional associations (the Evangelical Theological Society), and mission agencies focused on international and domestic efforts in gospel proclamation and humanitarian relief. These evangelicals also set out to reclaim an intellectual and academic voice in the broader culture, establishing new theological colleges and seminaries, Fuller Theological Seminary being the most notable among them at the time.[13]

But all this activity would have remained little more than a blip on the radar screen of American culture without the emergence of Billy Graham as a national celebrity.[14] Graham cut a wide swath in the American imagination. He called himself an "evangelical Christian" and, in no small measure, single-handedly gave that term the clear meaning the broader public and media had been seeking. Graham's willingness to work with those whom fundamentalists considered to be infidels—Roman Catholics and mainline Protestants at the head of that list—created the definitional separation from fundamentalism that this emerging rebirth of evangelicalism needed. By 1957 "fundamentalists had split irrevocably into two camps: neo-evangelicals versus militant separatists—or those who admired Graham versus those who thought he had left the fold."[15]

Graham's use of mass media and the media's fascination with him expanded the reach of his evangelistic meetings in ways never before imagined. His crusades attracted hundreds of thousands, and his media outreach touched millions. Graham became the twentieth-century George Whitefield, a celebrity preacher whose fame outstripped almost every other public figure, including most politicians, movie stars and recording artists. Graham's good looks, winsome smile, and humble manner gave evangelicalism the extreme makeover it desperately needed to regain credibility and a more appealing profile in the broader culture.

Through Graham's impetus, *Christianity Today*, evangelicalism's most widely read publication, was founded in 1956. Nearly every white Protestant pastor and ministry leader in the United States received copies of each edition. The intent of the magazine, according to its first editor, Carl F. H. Henry, was to carve out a distinct identity for evangelicals in the American religious landscape between liberal Protestantism, a movement he described as "adrift in speculation," and fundamentalism, which, he claimed, had failed to apply the whole gospel to the contemporary social crisis. Henry vowed that *Christianity Today* would be evangelicalism's "clear voice, to speak with conviction and love" into a world in crisis.[16] Evangelicals have attempted, with inconsistent results, to occupy and define the religious space between fundamentalists and mainline Protestants ever since.

Evangelicals are gospel people, and our commitment to evangelism remained strong in the last half of the twentieth century. Alongside the Billy Graham Evangelistic Association, parachurch ministries—Young Life, Youth for Christ, Campus Crusade for Christ, the Navigators, and InterVarsity Christian Fellowship among them—focused on evangelistic outreach among high school and college students. Media ministries, recording studios, broadcasting networks, and publishing houses rushed to meet the seemingly endless demand for evangelical radio and TV shows, Bible study materials, books, and music.

With respect to evangelism, an unresolved tension has plagued our movement since the late nineteenth century. How should God's people balance their commitments to gospel proclamation and social engagement? Published in 1947, Carl F. H. Henry's *The Uneasy Conscience of Modern Fundamentalism* captures the tension created by the fundamentalist assertion that biblical fidelity and gospel proclamation are not compatible with social engagement. "The evangelical task primarily is the preaching of the Gospel, in the interest of individual regeneration by the supernatural grace of God, in such a way that divine redemption can be recognized as the best solution of problems, individual and social. This produces within history, through the regenerative work of the Holy Spirit, a divine society that transcends national and international lines. The corporate testimony of believers, in their purity of life, should provide for the world an example of the divine dynamic to overcome evils in every realm."[17] Henry affirms that, as revivalist religion, evangelicals start with the premise that individual salvation is the foundation of societal transformation, a premise that the Puritans also held. The equation is simple and clear: the presence of saved and transformed individuals eventually translates into changed societies.

Unfortunately, our insistence that the starting point of social transformation is the spiritual regeneration of individual lives hasn't proved to be true. In fact, one could argue that it has allowed us to ignore systemic injustice and our own participation in its perpetuation while we were hard at work saving souls. Such was the case during the Jim Crow era in the South when segregation was simply accepted as "the way things are" and preached in many white churches as God ordained. And things didn't change much during the civil rights movement. Blending primitivism, political conservatism, white supremacy, and a literal reading of selected passages in the Bible, some evangelicals continued to propagate a folk theology that undergirded the ongoing cultural and legal protections needed for segregation to survive. By locating the "first problem" as individual sin and the "first solution" as individual salvation, many evangelicals continue to think of racism in a way that absolves most white people from participation in it and places the responsibility for the consequences of racism solely on the behavior and life choices of black people.[18]

American politics and revivalist religion may not seem likely bedfellows, but evangelicals have been involved in politics since the colonial era. As we saw earlier, they sometimes found themselves on opposite sides of issues. Some believed that the American Revolution was an act of rebellion against God. Others embraced freedom from the king as a gift from God. Some argued for the abolition of slavery; others believed that slavery was the God-ordained institution that he had providentially used to create the prosperity of the South. A few evangelicals marched to end segregation; others donned the robes and hoods of the Ku Klux Klan after attending church services. The civil rights movement in the 1960s brought this division vividly to the fore. Some conservative evangelicals condemned civil rights leaders, peaceful protests, and political activism to address racial inequality as the "devil's work." Many, even Graham at times in the early years of his public ministry, retreated to the position that individual salvation was the only way to address racism. That approach has proven to be naïve. To our shame, a lot of saved evangelicals have a mixed record in speaking out against white supremacy and racism. Theological education for the next evangelicalism must develop a thicker, richer theology of the cross and conversion in order for us to see how the power of the gospel can change not only individual lives but also communities and societies.

The constant refrain from fundamentalists and more conservative evangelicals in the middle years of the twentieth century had been that their mandate is to "preach the gospel" and not get entangled in politics. That seemed to be the position of the Reverend Jerry Falwell in a sermon he preached in March of 1965 entitled "Ministers and Marchers." Clearly questioning the faith and motives of civil rights leaders like Dr. Martin Luther King Jr. and denying that there was "discrimination against the Negro in the South," he proclaimed, "we are cognizant that our only purpose on this earth is to know Christ and to make Him known. Believing the Bible as I do, I would find it impossible to stop preaching the pure saving gospel of Jesus Christ, and begin doing anything else—including fighting Communism, or participating in civil-rights reforms."[19] Evidently, Falwell later had a conversion experience of a different sort than the kind experienced through the "pure saving gospel of Jesus Christ." Only a decade later he would preach, "The idea of 'religion and politics don't mix' was invented by the devil to keep Christians from running their own country."[20]

Evangelical political engagement intensified and became much more partisan from the late 1970s onward. Changes in the social, cultural, philosophical, and moral landscape that erupted in the 1960s and early 1970s threatened white evangelical assumptions, values, and lifestyle. So, we went to war again with the broader culture, fostering the same fear and indignation fundamentalist leaders played upon in the 1920s. Winning "culture wars" became our mission while "threatened and embattled minority" became our preferred identity. That same sense of mission and identity played out in evangelicalism after the election of Barack Obama in 2008 and remained central to evangelical support for Donald Trump, support that has remained in place even after he incited a violent insurrection against our very democracy. We just can't seem to move beyond the need to define ourselves more by the enemies we fear than by the hope we say we have in the gospel.

Flush with success in energizing a conservative evangelical voting bloc to defeat a professing evangelical president, Jimmy Carter, in the 1980 presidential election, Falwell's Moral Majority made evangelicalism and the Republican Party virtually indistinguishable from one another. From that time forward, the perception of evangelicals in the broader public has changed from being an essentially religious movement with involvement in politics to a nakedly partisan political movement run by religious conservatives. The unwavering and uncritical evangelical support for Donald Trump in the 2016 and 2020 presidential elections only confirms that shift in our public identity. No matter how much we want to see ourselves as "gospel people," that identity has been lost in the din of the partisan political bombast of some evangelical leaders with large media followings. We face no greater dilemma and challenge than the loss of our identity and mission as people of the gospel. The next evangelicalism must create a meaningful public theology and prophetic presence centered upon and defined by what we say matters most to us—the gospel of Jesus Christ in its fullest expression.

Another issue in the contentious process of evangelicals trying to distinguish themselves from fundamentalists and regain credibility in the broader culture emerges at the intersection of science and faith. Both groups agreed that God created "the heavens and the earth." But they could not agree on how God had done that. Adam Laats describes the different approaches of the two groups. "[Evangelical scientists] insisted that evolutionary science—properly understood—was also God's science. Real Christianity and real creationism meant understanding real science in its true beauty and complexity. Fundamentalist scientists offered a different answer.... Only young-earth creationism, they insisted, was real creationism. Anything else was an apostasy, a world-pleasing liberalism that greased the path to perdition."[21] Although not all fundamentalists painted liberalism in such extreme terms, many used the "slippery slope" meme to warn that accepting evolutionary science would ultimately lead to a denial of the rest of the Bible.

The relationship between faith and science was not problematic for most evangelical leaders before the rise of fundamentalism. These evangelicals embraced scientific developments with little sense that doing so conflicted with their faith commitments.[22] That posture changed dramatically in the early twentieth century as fundamentalist leaders began to promote the same view that had been prosecuted by atheistic scientists in the late nineteenth century in the United Kingdom, namely, that faith and science were "at war" with one another. Science became the enemy of faith, and the faithful were warned of its insidious agenda to undermine all that fundamentalists held sacred. The idea that the scientific community and, indeed, the entire secular academic community are at war with the believing community retains a powerful presence among fundamentalists and conservative evangelicals today. When that suspicion is politicized, as in the case of climate science, for example, many evangelicals simply refuse to acknowledge the veracity of the data that the scientific community embraces. When fundamentalists "go to war" against the scientific community, they force the faithful to make a choice between science and faith, a choice that many younger evangelicals make at the expense of their faith.

Our commonly held biblicism and instinctive primitivism continue to spawn many of the controversies and recriminations that fly between evangelicals and fundamentalists. While both sides confess belief in the inspired, inerrant, and authoritative text of Scripture, we often disagree about how the Bible addresses contemporary intellectual, ethical, and sociocultural questions that biblical authors and previous generations of like-minded Bible readers did not face. The ostensible flashpoint in these disagreements is the doctrine of biblical inerrancy. The pattern of the conflict is typically the more conservative side accusing others of denying inerrancy if they come to a different conclusion on the interpretation of a passage or application of it to contemporary realities. For some, biblical inerrancy remains a weapon in the battle to define the boundaries of the movement. Frequently, however, the real issue isn't the inerrant nature of the text but the tendency we have to consider our own interpretations and applications of a text inerrant, a problem that has bedeviled evangelicalism since the earliest days of the Evangelical Theological Society (ETS).[23]

Regardless of the ways that inerrancy has been misused to create conflict among evangelicals, it remains a foundational conviction in the movement. The battle over inerrancy is a "proxy war" in the much larger conflict between faith and reason as sources of intellectual authority.[24] For most evangelicals, "the concept of a deeply flawed or errant Scripture is a virtual oxymoron."[25] The stakes are too high and the cost too severe for the next evangelicalism to move away from inerrancy. Theological education for the next evangelicalism has an opportunity to reconceptualize and rearticulate what we believe about the truthfulness and authority of the Bible so that the movement reengages the text in ways that its power, relevance, and authority are brought to the fore. Our primary task is not to defend the Bible but to embrace it and live by it in such a compelling way that everyone who knows us will want to know the God it reveals.

The future of evangelical theological education seems as uncertain as the future of evangelicalism itself. Although those of us who lead its schools wake up every morning concerned about institutional questions like viability and sustainability, the most pressing concerns are much more visceral and fearsome. Will evangelicalism as we've known it find a way to unite around the convictions and virtues that are woven through its history? Or will it continue to fracture on the fault lines of its vices and anxieties? Perhaps our history as a reactionary, revivalist renewal movement provides more of an answer to those questions than we're willing to admit. We have reinvented ourselves before, and the need to do so again could not be more acute. I pray that we are on the cusp of the next great period of agitation and change that will carve out the next evangelicalism as a movement defined by the hope of the gospel for the world.

The next evangelicalism must be grounded theologically and hermeneutically or it simply cannot claim to be evangelical. But can we as theological educators create the kind of theological engagement and learning needed to help ground the next evangelicalism? That's the challenge we face. Theological education for the next evangelicalism faces the daunting and exhilarating task of calling the movement to be its "best self" more consistently and thoroughly. Thinking about that task will occupy our attention in the remainder of this book.

– Future Matters –

Dear Ellie, Brett, Sofia, Anna, and Justin,

Truly great stories do far more than entertain. They transform us. And it is often the case that the meaning of truly great stories becomes evident only as we come to the end of them. I still remember the moment near the conclusion of Shūsāku Endo's Silence: A Novel *when the story's meaning, indeed even its title, startled me with its profundity and poignance.*

We live in the middle of a story whose meaning we already know because its end is already revealed. So we live in the magnificent privilege of biblical hope—redemption accomplished, the promise of life in its fullness awaits. Our vision of that certain future guides our vision for theological education. Redemption, restoration, justice, life, healing, joy—these are the theologically rich images that ought to drive theological education for the next evangelicalism.

Don't be afraid to allow your yearning for the brokenness of this world to be healed in the hope of future redemption to shape the schools you lead. Educating God's people for the sake of the world will require changes in institutional forms, programs, faculty composition, and the way we think about the theological priorities that define us. That kind of change feels dangerous because it threatens comfort and complacency. There will be opposition, even suffering,

perhaps. That's what Jesus promised his disciples if they were to fol-
low him toward the vision of redemption he so masterfully laid out
before them.

The past matters, but the future matters more. By this I do not
mean that we have the luxury of ignoring, forgetting, or rewriting
our past. Our past lays down the limitations and the possibilities of
our present and future. It provides meaning that can be gleaned no-
where else. But it doesn't give us the full meaning. The full meaning
of the present becomes clear in the collision of an honest memory and
hopeful vision. We are called as educators to glean meaning for our
present by harvesting truth from both our past and our future.

Don't lose hope as you yearn for the future laid before us, the re-
demption of all things, and strive to make it ever more real through
the presence of God's people. Our movement needs a fresh vision of
that future. Our world needs the hope that what they yearn for can
be theirs in Christ.

Prayerful for you,

Mark

7

Bible

Forever etched in my memory, this little ditty was sung just about every week in Sunday school when I was a kid:

> The B-I-B-L-E,
> yes, that's the book for me!
> I stand alone on the Word of God,
> the B-I-B-L-E, the Bible.

With millions of views on YouTube, it seems to be enjoying a long shelf life in evangelical churches. That one line, "I stand alone on the Word of God," says more about the history and nature of evangelicalism than any child could ever realize. It captures our biblicism and our individualism, two cherished and at times problematic values in American evangelicalism.

We are people of the Book, believing the Bible to be our final authority for faith and practice. That's a *sine qua non* for evangelicals. That conviction defines us and shapes us. We study the Bible with both reverence and reason, looking to it as our authoritative reference point, assessing theories and arguments by their congruence with what it affirms. We read the Bible to find hope and encouragement in a fallen world. We marvel at its intricacies and revel in its simplicity. We meditate on it and contemplate how profoundly it describes us even though written millennia ago. We read it as both time-stamped and timeless. In the Bible we find God's solution for our sins and his salve for our wounds. We seek God's wisdom in the Bible and strive to align our behavior with what we find. We preach and teach the Bible. We sing it, recite it, memorize it, and constantly find ourselves looking to it for truth that endures.

Perhaps more so than any other major Christian group, we evangelicals are known for our commitment to studying the Bible. Evangelical biblical scholars do research and publish in leading academic journals and symposia. We buy more Bible commentaries, reference books, and study guides than any other Protestant group. We take the Bible seriously; we take our privilege to study it seriously; and we take our responsibility to think and live under its authority seriously. Moreover, because we value it so highly, evangelicals have taken the lead in translating the Bible into the languages of some of the most isolated people groups on the planet. Those efforts have brought literacy programs to people neglected, forgotten, or unknown by those in power in the lands where they live. Our drive to make the Bible available to all persons on the planet in a language they speak with fluency reveals just how much we value its presence and believe in its power to change lives, communities, even societies.

As revivalist religion, evangelicalism is also populist religion. The prospect of a populist biblicism was inconceivable, if not terrifying, to the hierarchy of the Roman Catholic Church at the time of the Reformation. Many clergy feared that if each individual believer were taught to read and interpret Scripture apart from the authority of the church, religious chaos would ensue. And, in a sense, they were right. Alongside the spiritual renewal and life-giving freedom that greater access to the Bible brought to northern and central Europe, it also exacerbated the fragmentation of Christian thought, practice, and community in early Protestantism. With no single authoritative hermeneutic or ecclesiastical arbiter of biblical truth, various interpretations of texts and church doctrines gained traction and formed the foundations for new denominational and theological identities. Although some Protestant groups took their hermeneutical and theological differences all the way to the battlefield, most have been able to find enough common ground in their reading of Scripture to maintain a remarkably resilient cohesiveness in their theological priorities. Mark Noll uses the phrase "chaotic coherence"[1] to describe the surprising, if not miraculous, consistency in the core beliefs of evangelicals through what at times has seemed like a genetic predisposition to divisive squabbles and denominational splits between groups that interpret passages and articulate beliefs differently.

Biblicism functions as a value, a belief, and a practice in evangelicalism. In its simplest and most powerful form, it means that we see the Bible as our final authority for faith and practice. That affirmation leads to the assumptions that we can understand the Bible and that we must obey its teaching. These convictions, in turn, lead to the widespread practice of daily Bible reading and intentional study of biblical texts. Although there are variations among evangelicals in the ways we live out our commitment to biblicism, it remains a foundation of our movement.

Yes, we love the Bible.

And yet, we have a biblicism problem. Not a Bible problem and not a bibliology problem. Our biblicism becomes a problem when we read the Bible too simplistically, interpret it too arrogantly, and apply it too selectively.

We believe the Bible is inspired by God and is therefore without error in what it affirms. Its authority, we assert, rests upon the very character of God. Most evangelicals also affirm that the Bible's meaning is "plain," that it is understandable as written. This conviction gives us confidence that each of us can interpret the Bible and benefit from its teaching. And that's true. Yet, significant, long-standing, and seemingly irresolvable differences in the interpretation of some passages among those who hold these convictions in common have prompted some to raise serious questions about biblicism.[2] If the Bible is understandable and clear, why do we come up with different interpretations of the same passage? Furthermore, the meaning of some passages is notoriously difficult to discern, no matter the level of one's hermeneutical skills. We may be tempted to ask, "Just how 'plain' is the meaning of the Bible?"

These questions relate far more to our unwillingness to acknowledge the complexity of the Bible and our limitations in interpreting it than to the nature of the Bible itself. At its worst, biblicism can lead us to ignore the literary character, theological grounding, narrative framing, and cultural locatedness of a text. In our conviction that the meaning of the Bible is plain and accessible to all, we tend to downplay just how complex interpreting it really is. If we're not keenly aware of our own finitude and cultural locatedness in interpreting the Bible, biblicism can lead to an unwarranted certainty, even dogmatism, that our interpretation of even disputed passages is the only correct way to understand them. Hermeneutical arrogance creates an unwillingness to admit that if people with common theological commitments and equally competent exegetical practices have not been able to agree on the interpretation of particular passages for generations, the conclusions we draw about the meaning and significance of those passages must be approached with intellectual honesty and humility. Unfortunately, a lack of such humility has added to our movement's propensity toward bruising internal conflict and schism.

Even when we agree on the interpretation of a passage, we may differ on how to live out its truth. For some, attaching the adjective "biblical" to the life application of a passage means that everyone, everywhere needs to adopt the same behaviors if they want to live under the authority of Scripture. In some cases that is true and helpful. In others, however, particularly when contextual differences are ignored, it can be quite problematic. Even more problematic is the widespread practice of demanding a literal interpretation and life application of some biblical texts while giving far less credence to, or flat out ignoring, the teaching and ethical demands of many others. Some biblical passages, it seems, have more authority than others in evangelicalism. Although loath to admit it, we treat selected verses of the Bible as a more authoritative canon within the accepted canon of Scripture.

The bottom line is this: in spite of a long-standing love affair with the Bible, our biblicism has not kept us from our current identity crisis. In fact, among some evangelicals, it has facilitated it. Just as the biblicism of the nineteenth century failed to unify evangelicals in opposition to race-based slavery and to expose the assumption of white supremacy that undergirded it, our approach to the Bible today has failed to unify the movement around our gospel identity and to expose the idolatries that undergird our pursuit of political power. In more than one way our biblicism has failed us, and theological education for the next evangelicalism must challenge the movement to consider it afresh.

The importance and the risk of taking on this task should not be underestimated. It steps on sacred turf for evangelicals. Nothing sets off alarm bells and raises our hackles more quickly than a perceived threat to or deviation from the way we read, interpret, and apply the Bible. But theological education for the next evangelicalism must help us rethink the way we read, interpret, and live out the authority of the Bible if we desire to renew our gospel-centric identity and mission for the sake of the world.

Reading the Bible

Everyone starts somewhere when they read the Bible. Before we open its pages, we assume certain things about Scripture's character and nature. Those assumptions shape our approach to reading it. Many evangelicals see the Bible as a handbook containing wisdom and guidance for every area of life. Many see the Bible as a rule book that focuses more on our failures than on our virtues, while still others view it as a guidebook mapping out the events of the future. These approaches make the Bible out to be far less than it was written to be.

The Bible is much more than a handbook, a rule book, and a guidebook. The Bible is a story that claims to be the one true story of the one true God's engagement in human history. As such, it is an epic saga that spans human history, lays bare human nature, and reveals human destiny. More than a collection of helpful tips, ideas, or predictions, the Bible is a story.[3]

It's in our DNA to love a great story. "The human mind is a story processor, not a logic processor."[4] That's why stories shape our thinking and our values more than logical arguments and bulleted lists of facts. Through stories we "connect the dots" of perceptions, data, findings, arguments, feelings, values, and experiences.

All of us live by some story that helps us answer life's most important questions. We live by that story, even though we may not be conscious we are doing so. We also love by it. We might even be asked to die for it. We're often unaware of the story we live by until we encounter and explore other people's stories. Because our story influences us so deeply, we all need to ask a question many may feel far too intimidating to consider seriously, namely, "Is the story by which I live true?"

Every culture has its own collection of stories. Some of them—often those expressed in religious traditions—create our identities and shape our deepest values. By its very nature, religion claims to make sense and give meaning to reality, both immanent and ultimate. Most religions, whether formal or folk, create a shared sense of past, present, and future through stories that are told generation after generation. These stories shape the way we think about the nature of spiritual realities, the nature of humanity, and the interaction between the spiritual and physical realms. As we learn and repeat our own history, our own stories, we deepen our sense of identity.

British theologian Lesslie Newbigin, who lived as a missionary in South India for much of his adult life, notes that "The way we understand human life depends on what conception we have of the human story."[5] The Bible is that kind of life-shaping story. Newbigin goes on to say that the Bible, as universal history, tells the whole story of the world from beginning to end. And every other story is at best only a partial telling of the true story of the world.

> If we take the Bible in its canonical wholeness, as we must, then it is best understood as history. It is universal, cosmic history. It interprets the entire story of all things from creation to consummation, and the story of the human race within creation, and

within the human race the story of the people of God to be the
bearers of the meaning of the whole, and—at the very centre—the
story of the One in whom God's purpose was decisively revealed
by being decisively effected. It is obviously a different story from
the stories the world tells about itself.[6]

The Bible claims to be *the* one true story. It claims to be the story
that fills in the gaps in all other stories and provides correction
to errors they may contain.

That is an audacious claim and, in a pluralistic world, an of-
fensive one. Knowing that there are many competing stories by
which people make sense of the world and find their own sense
of purpose in it, we might be tempted to think that the Bible is
irrelevant in a world like ours, so completely out of step with
modern sensibilities that it can't possibly be what it claims to
be. But we have to remember that when the Bible was composed,
both in the ancient Near East and in first-century Greco-Roman
culture, the world was already full of other stories. The authors
of all the books of the Bible lived in contexts that were just as
pluralistic as our world today. Yet the authors of the Bible never
shy away from, never back down from, the claim that the Bible
tells the one true story of the one true God and his involvement
in human history. And neither must the next evangelicalism, no
matter how uncomfortable or unacceptable that claim may be
in the broader culture.

The Bible is a big story. It addresses the big questions by which
people live but about which they may not talk explicitly, questions like: Is there a God? What does it mean to be human? What
is the meaning of life? Where can we find hope for the future?
The Bible begs the reader to ask those same questions and invites
the reader to find answers in its story. Newbigin describes how
the Bible addresses these life-shaping questions: "To be human
is to be a part of a story, and to be fully human as God intends
is to be part of the true story and to understand its beginning
and its ending. The true story is one of which the central clues
are given in the Bible, and the hinge of the story on which all

its meaning turns is the incarnation, death, and resurrection of Jesus Christ. That is the message we are entrusted with, and we owe it to all people to share it."[7]

Seeing the Bible as the universally true story and our faith as a unique way of framing human history with Jesus as the interpretive key provides the basis upon which evangelicals relate to the other stories by which people live. Not seeing the Bible as that one true story creates the tragic inevitability that we will live by another story, often dressed up in language from the Bible but essentially at odds with its truth and values. Living by another story leads to the subversion of our faith,[8] an undermining of our identity and witness through the pursuit of the values of that other story. The current crisis in evangelicalism betrays our movement's subversion of the biblical story through the adoption of counternarratives replete with Christian terms and distorted Christian truth. What a tragedy. Only we, the church, can tell the story of Jesus and live into it with integrity. That story is our identity. Our mission is to "tell this story as clearly as possible, and to allow it to subvert other ways of telling the story of the world."[9]

The Bible, our story, is a redemption story. It narrates the good news of God's great redemptive work by which he rescues all creation from sin, death, and evil and restores it to the fullness of life. The centerpiece of the story is the Christ event—the incarnation, death, and resurrection of Jesus. Like the neck of an hourglass, everything in the story flows into it and then out from it. The Christ event is the interpretive point of reference from which the rest of the biblical story derives its meaning. For evangelicals, Jesus, therefore, is rightly seen as the "decisive clue" to understanding all of human history.[10]

As a redemption story, the Bible is a story of hope: hope deferred, hope embodied, and hope made certain. The beginning of the story foreshadows its end. In both, God dwells with his people in perfect harmony and they enjoy his good creation without encumbrance. Between the beginning and the end, however, the story baldly exposes humanity's rebellion and the horrific consequences of their sin. Sin, death, and evil terrorize and brutalize all creation, including humanity, God's image-bearers. But throughout the story, no matter how horrifically the chthonic trio—sin, death, and evil—mar the beauty of creation, pervert justice, fracture relationships, and distort the essence of life, the hope of redemption is always present. God cannot, does not, and will not abandon his people. He intervenes and redeems, rescuing them from the full consequences of their rebellion and restoring them to the place of his promise. God's redemptive acts in the Old Testament point to the end of the story by pointing the reader to Jesus, announcing redemption, accomplishing redemption on the cross, confirming redemption in the resurrection, and ultimately consummating redemption when all creation is made new. That's a story worth living into and living out.

The story of the Bible never loses sight of its climactic final chapters. Even though it may seem to lose its way at times, the story keeps moving toward the end God has ordained. Like the course of the Mississippi River, which winds back and forth with seemingly little sense of pattern but is always moving toward the Gulf of Mexico, the Bible keeps pushing toward the end it foresees and promises. And that matters. We typically cannot discern the meaning of a story, or even whether there is a meaning, until we reach its conclusion. But the story of the Bible is different. Its end has been revealed in the middle through the person of Jesus Christ.[11] Our privilege is to live in the middle of the story, knowing how it will end. That's the hope of the gospel, the certainty that Jesus is making all things new and will complete his redemptive work in the restoration of all things. That hope gives meaning to our lives; it is the hope that sets the Christian story apart. And as the people of that story, it sets us on mission.

Theological education for the next evangelicalism must be conceived and imbued with the startling claim that the Bible is cosmic history, that Jesus is the centerpiece of that history, and that our faith is a unique telling of it. Every program, course, learning outcome, and assignment must be framed by that story in order to cement our identity and mission in it. This approach will elevate biblical studies from its place as one discipline in the curriculum to an overarching framework for the rest of the curriculum. Such an approach to the theological curriculum makes it possible for the next evangelicalism to move beyond the facile approaches to the Bible—handbook, rule book, guidebook—that have crippled so much of our movement today and experience the Bible's unique power to shape us.

A more nuanced, theologically framed, and narratively focused biblicism must undergird the content, curricula, outcomes, and mission of theological education for the next evangelicalism. In that way, theologically trained pastors can help our movement define and express itself through the story of God's great work of redemption. Telling and living that story is the most powerful way to establish our identity and regain our credibility as people of the gospel in the generations ahead.

Living the Bible

In his profound and sometimes hilarious book *The Year of Living Biblically: One Man's Humble Quest to Follow the Bible as Literally as Possible*, A. J. Jacobs poignantly describes the impossibility of obeying all the Bible's commands literally in contemporary society. And most evangelicals would agree. It's impossible to obey all the commands of the Bible literally. But that impossibility raises questions that have bedeviled our movement for centuries: "Which biblical commands should we obey literally?" "Which ones should we obey by adopting similar behaviors?" and "Which ones can we ignore?"

These questions aren't just academic. They have tremendous power to shape behavior and relationships. When my wife and I lived in the Soviet bloc, it was common for the men in some of the older Russian Protestant churches to greet one another with a kiss on the lips. In Poland, some of the older male believers kissed one another three times on alternating cheeks. The practice of greeting with a kiss was their literal application of Paul's and Peter's exhortations in the New Testament to "greet one another with a holy kiss."[12] In the many evangelical churches I have visited in the United States, I have never seen that practice followed. In its stead, we shake hands, evidently believing that greeting ritual to be a sufficient substitute for the biblical command to greet with a kiss. On other behaviors described, prescribed, and proscribed in the Bible, however, we take a much more literal approach. For example, in some evangelical churches, women are not allowed to teach or preach in settings where men are present because of a literal application of the apostle Paul's statement in 1 Timothy 2:11–12, "A woman should learn in quietness and full submission. I do not permit a woman to teach or to assume authority over a man; she must be quiet." Unfortunately, many evangelicals argue that those who do not agree with their application of this Pauline practice of prohibiting women from teaching men are denying the authority of Scripture or, in some cases, their allegiance to the gospel. That's a serious and sad accusation given the exegetical, theological, and contextual evidence marshaled by those who live out the authority of this passage in ways that support women teaching and preaching in communities of faith. Our inconsistent approach to applying biblical passages to our lives creates significant, often acrimonious, divisions in our movement. It also undermines our credibility in the broader culture.

Because we see the Bible as the source of universally true propositions about God and universally valid principles for godly living, we use the adjective "biblical" broadly and often.[13] However, we do not seem to use it consistently and with serious regard for the complexity of what it may mean hermeneutically and how it relates to life application. For example, what do we mean by phrases like "biblical marriage," "biblical child-rearing," "biblical money management," and "biblical leadership"? We do the same for dozens of other areas of human experience as well. In many cases, "biblical" simply means that a statement, value, or behavior in a given contemporary context mirrors or resembles selected statements, values, and behaviors found in a text of Scripture. Yet, for every behavior we label as "biblical" in our contemporary setting, there are dozens more in the Bible that seemingly are not "biblical" in our setting.

Once we apply the label "biblical" to a behavior, we typically consider it to be universally applicable. Unfortunately, this approach to the Bible often leads to an ethnocentric elevation of the interpreter's values and behaviors as "biblical" based on a selection of those passages in Scripture that more closely mirror already acceptable behaviors in the interpreter's culture. Such was the hermeneutical approach taken by some evangelicals to justify race-based slavery, Jim Crow injustice, and segregation. Many of those who participated in the slave trade contended that the enslavement of trafficked Africans in America was biblical because the Bible sanctioned slavery in the Old Testament and did not prohibit it in the New.

Conversely, passages containing behaviors that are alien to the interpreter's own cultural setting or challenge ways of life that the interpreter cannot imagine surrendering are often simply ignored. These passages, and the behaviors they contain, are often dubbed "cultural," as opposed to biblical. This designation means the behaviors were authoritative in the time and place in which they were written by the biblical author but are not authoritative for the interpreter's context and faith community. Through this very convenient labeling system the passages deemed "cultural" do not carry the same authority in our lives as other passages. Through this approach we create our "canon within the canon."

We have to admit, therefore, that in our common approach to applying Scripture, some parts of the Bible have more authority than others. But that admission contradicts our professed belief that the Bible, all of it, is the final authority in our faith and practice. A pressing question for theological educators in the next evangelicalism is, "How must we rethink our hermeneutic so that we more intentionally and consistently live out our commitment to the authority of *all* Scripture?"

Approaching the Bible as the cosmic history of redemption centered on the Christ event establishes a foundation for such a hermeneutic. If we assume that the purpose of the Bible is to reveal, in the radically pluralistic contexts of its origin, the person of the one true God and his redemptive purpose, then we must read every passage with that purpose in mind. Since the Christ event—Jesus's life, death, resurrection, and ascension—is the centerpiece of the story, and, since the end of the story—the consummation of redemption when Jesus returns—is already revealed, all passages should be interpreted and applied in light of that framework.

Two questions dominate the interpretive task: "What do the behaviors, values, and teachings in any given passage reveal about the one true God in the context in which they were given?" and "How do these behaviors, values, and teachings create a clear testimony of his redemptive work and purpose in that context?" The answers to those questions create the foundation for interpreters to identify and articulate principles for faithful application of passages based on a serious linguistic, literary, theological, and sociocultural examination of each passage in its original setting. These questions require us to move through the *what* question to the *why* and *how* questions when interpreting the Bible. "Why did the biblical author command God's people to live this way in that setting?" "How does this way of life reveal God's redemptive work and purpose for all people?"

Through culturally sensitive exegesis of the context of the biblical passage and the interpreter's own contemporary context, we have the privilege and responsibility then to articulate the truth of every passage of Scripture and live under its authority in such a way that the character of our God and the redemptive work of Christ are communicated in a credible and compelling way. When we shape our behavior to reveal the character of Jesus and to testify to the redemptive power of the gospel, we can confidently speak of living "biblically." In some instances, our application of a passage may parallel the behaviors described in the original setting. In other cases, living out the authority of a passage may require behaviors that differ from the original. To return to our earlier example, in some contemporary settings a kiss of greeting may neither reveal the character of Jesus nor create a compelling testimony of his redemptive work. In these cases, a believing community can determine what behaviors in their contemporary setting will reveal the same truths about Jesus and his redemptive work as the kiss of greeting did in the first-century Greco-Roman world. In other contemporary cultures and faith communities, a kiss of greeting may in fact beautifully express the character and redemptive work of Jesus, just as it did in the first century.

This approach to interpreting and applying the Bible can only be accomplished communally, and only when a faith community is willing to embrace diverse voices. Restoring the role of the broader faith community in hermeneutical practice and missional application will require a jarring departure from the typically individualistic, white, male-dominant approach to biblical interpretation and application in evangelical theological education. As New Testament professor Dan Wallace has noted, "Ever since the days of the Princetonians (Hodge, Warfield, Machen, et al.), American non-charismatic evangelicalism has been dominated by Scottish Common Sense, post-Enlightenment, left-brain, obsessive-compulsive, white males. This situation reveals that we are suppressing a part of the image of God, suppressing a part of the witness of the Spirit, and that we are not in line with historic Christianity."[14] The ever-growing presence of male and female biblical scholars from diverse backgrounds in evangelical schools bodes well for the next evangelicalism. Theological education must continue to drive this development through ever-greater dependence upon diverse voices in the fields of biblical and theological studies.

The next evangelicalism must embrace the privilege and responsibility of creating diverse communities of practice through which our biblicism can be expressed in new forms, diligently studying Scripture to understand how the character of God and the redemptive power of the gospel are revealed in biblical settings and then courageously assessing our own context to discern what behaviors, values, and teachings reveal the same today. Evangelical communities of faith living in two distinct contexts may live out the authority of a given passage of Scripture differently, and yet both approaches can be considered consistent with our commitment to the authority of Scripture. Moreover, the next evangelicalism must practice the humility needed to look beyond differences in the interpretation and application of Scripture to life that inhibit us from keeping the hope-filled gospel at the center of our identity.

We often say that the Bible is written *for* God's people. Perhaps we need to tweak our perspective and language a bit and affirm that the Bible is written *to* God's people *for* the sake of the world. Yes, it shapes us and leads us into a life that can only be found in Christ. But that wonderful gift is never just for our sakes. When read as the story of redemption through the lens of the Christ event, the Bible becomes intensely missional, and the faith community's motivation for creating a true testimony of the one true God in their own culture through their beliefs, values, and practices drives the hermeneutical task. "Biblical" then takes on a more expansive meaning that gives each faith community a sense of their privileged role in the great story of the Bible and the grand purpose of God. It also gives us a humble awareness of our own cultural limitations in interpretation and application. And that realization gives urgency and rationale to each faith community in the task of contextualization.

Theological education for the next evangelicalism must rethink biblicism so that our faith communities have the framework, impetus, and agency to live in ways that attest to the character of Jesus, the dignity of all people, and the redemptive power of the gospel above all else. With that mission in mind, our identity as people of the gospel can emerge from the fog and din created by our dalliance with the gods of politics and power for the past fifty years.

Such a vision for theological education demands that we rethink the place and role of biblical studies in our curricula. We don't need less Bible in our programs. We need more. But not in the same way that our biblicism has shaped theological curricula in the past. The number of credit hours that carries an institution's curricular prefix for biblical studies courses isn't the problem or the solution. Framing the entire curriculum with the story of Scripture, enriching every area of learning with the knowledge of Scripture, and guiding students toward learning outcomes that express the authority of Scripture remain the foundation of evangelical theological education. Framing and enriching a curriculum that guides students to learning outcomes that express the authority of Scripture requires more than prooftexting and casual allusions to the Bible. It requires deep and rich integrated biblical studies, including instruction in biblical languages, that reinforce the hermeneutical framework of Scripture as cosmic history, the one true story of God's redemptive mission, in every academic discipline. In this way, biblical studies can help address, in conversation with those both inside and outside the faith, the most pressing and disquieting questions of life in a broken and messy world. Breaking down traditional disciplinary and departmental walls, an integrated approach to biblical studies will nurture a nuanced, theologically enriched understanding of what it means for the people of God's mission to live out the authority of all Scripture in every area of life so that we create a credible and compelling testimony of the gospel. That's theological education for the sake of the world. It's the theological education that will ground the next evangelicalism's identity in the hope of the gospel.

Cross

My grandma used to say, "You can tell a lot about a man by the songs he sings." If that's true (and who would ever dare disagree with Grandma?), we evangelicals see the cross at the center of our faith. An untold number of hymns, choruses, and contemporary praise songs draw our minds and hearts to the death of Jesus Christ on the cross. We sing them just about every time we gather. And they come to our lips easily and freely when our thoughts turn to faith.

There is no Christian faith without the cross. Moreover, there can be no expression of evangelicalism without the cross at the center of its theology. But the question we have to ask ourselves in these days is whether we are known for this commitment to the cross in the broader culture. Does our social identity, defined more by our politics than by our theology, express the beliefs, values, and behaviors that a crucicentric faith and cruciform life demand? Tragically, it does not. Theological education for the next evangelicalism must rearticulate crucicentrism in ways that lead us to a more cruciform presence in the world.

The Centrality of the Cross

In 1 Corinthians 2:2, the apostle Paul writes, "For I resolved to know nothing while I was with you except Jesus Christ and him crucified." Knowing that the apostle talked about many different issues with the Corinthians, this statement strikes an odd chord. Perhaps Martin Luther's famous dicta, "The cross alone is our theology" (*Crux sola est nostra theologia*) and "The cross tests everything" (*Crux probat omnia*), show us a way forward in understanding what the apostle meant: the cross is the central reference point of Christian theology. It frames and gives meaning to all our theological affirmations. David Bebbington summarizes the historical centrality of the crucifixion in evangelical thought, "To make any theme other than the cross the fulcrum of a theological system was to take a step away from Evangelicalism."[1]

Luther's statements about the cross profoundly challenge the way we and the broader society think about God. But there's more yet to say about the significance of the crucifixion. It also frames and gives meaning to human history. Fleming Rutledge beautifully expresses this startling claim:

> *The crucifixion is the touchstone of Christian authenticity, the unique feature by which everything else, including the resurrection, is given its true significance.* The resurrection is not a set piece. It is not an isolated demonstration of divine dazzlement. It is not to be detached from its abhorrent first act. The resurrection is, precisely, the vindication of a man who was crucified. Without the cross at the center of the Christian proclamation, the Jesus story can be treated as just another story about a charismatic spiritual figure. It is the crucifixion that marks out Christianity as something definitively different in the history of religion. *It is in the crucifixion that the nature of God is truly revealed.* Since the resurrection is God's mighty transhistorical Yes to the historically crucified Son, we can assert that *the crucifixion is the most important historical event that has ever happened.*[2]

Many may dismiss as religious hyperbole the assertion that the crucifixion of Jesus Christ is the "most important historical event that has ever happened," but one could not do so and remain faithful to evangelical identity and theology.

We believe that by his death on the cross, Jesus accomplishes redemption and changes the arc of human history and human

88

destiny. Through his death on the cross, Jesus defeats the unholy trinity—sin, death, and evil—that has plagued humanity since the beginning of time. That's why Paul can assert that the cross is the dividing point for all humanity. Every human's identity is defined in relationship to the cross, and every human's destiny is shaped by it (1 Cor. 1:18). That being the case, not only our theology but also our lives and ministries must be centered on the cross. This exhortation, delivered to Methodist pastors and leaders in 1892, expresses that sentiment well: "Give to the death of Christ its true place in your own experience and in your Christian work—as a witness to the real and profound evil of sin, as an overwhelming manifestation of Divine love, as the ground of acceptance with God, as a pattern of sacrifice to disturb us when life is too easy, to inspire and console us when life is hard, and as the only effectual appeal to the general heart of men, and, above all, as the Atonement for our sins."[3] If the cross centers evangelicalism theologically and missionally, it must also center our theological education.

The Offer of Heaven

As revivalist religion, evangelicalism sings its most familiar song in the offer of forgiveness for sin, newness of life, peace with God, and the hope of heaven, all of which are made possible by Jesus's death on the cross. No evangelical has embodied that message and proclaimed it to more people than Billy Graham. His clear, concise, and compelling presentation of the gospel preached thousands of times to millions of people worldwide and summarized in his book *Peace with God*[4] is still held dear by the vast majority of evangelicals. The cross stands at the center of Graham's theology and gospel appeal, which typically unfolds in three movements. First, all of us are sinners deserving judgment and in need of forgiveness. Second, because of his love for us, God sent his Son to pay the penalty for our sin by dying on the cross in our place. And third, when we believe that Jesus did just that and ask him to forgive our sins, we are born again, enter into a personal relationship with God, and receive the certainty that when we die we will spend eternity with him in heaven. The death of Jesus on the cross functions as the axial theme of our relationship with God, which we almost always narrate in three chapters: "before the cross," "at the cross," and "after the cross." This is boilerplate evangelical theology and testimony.

Our view of the crucifixion is intensely personal and essentially transactional. The belief that "because of his great love for *me*, Jesus died on the cross for *me*" adds a deep emotional layer to the faith of evangelicals. We not only believe in Jesus, we love Jesus because of what he has done for us. Viewing the crucifixion as a personal act of love is powerfully formative and motivating. It allows us to speak naturally of having a personal relationship with God that brings a sense of personal worth and security. This experience distinguishes evangelicalism from many other expressions of Christian faith, and it remains central to our identity. I'm afraid that many evangelicals don't know just how unusual this language sounds to most people, both religious and secular. Yet, for evangelicals, its effect is both liberating and empowering. There can be no religious movement called evangelical without an emphasis on this personal, emotionally satisfying, and transformative relationship with Jesus.

A transactional view of the crucifixion fits our penchant as Americans to use metaphors from the world of commerce in almost every area of life, including our theology of the cross. We are in good company doing so. New Testament authors also used business terms to describe the theological meaning of the crucifixion. Paul's phrasing "you were *bought* at a price" (1 Cor. 6:20; 7:23) and John's description of angelic beings praising the crucified and resurrected Christ in the heavenly throne room for having "*purchased* for God persons from every tribe and language and people and nation" (Rev. 5:9) serve as examples. A transactional view of the crucifixion also accommodates the language of substitution and atonement. "He died in our place to pay the price for our sin" is common parlance in evangelicalism. In exchange for that price, we receive something—the forgiveness of sin, newness of life, peace with God, and the assurance of everlasting life in heaven. Transactional metaphors communicate powerfully because we use them every day in common discourse. We pay a price and get something in return. The value proposition of revivalist religion is pretty simple: someone paid the price for you to have what you desperately want but could never purchase on your own, a ticket to heaven. That's a good deal!

This personal, transactional approach to the crucifixion creates a spiritual silo within which the marvelous spiritual benefits of having a relationship with God are enjoyed. What happens in the silo, the resolution of our sin problem and renewal of our souls, stays in the silo. If the ultimate benefit of the crucifixion is the forgiveness of an individual's sins and the certainty of eternity in heaven, what difference does it make in the world? Evidently, very little. Although I've heard many evangelistic sermons with appeals to each person to repent, believe in the death of Christ as the payment for sin, and know with certainty that forgiveness is given and heaven will be gained, those appeals always focus only on individual sins. Sexual promiscuity, lying, and greed top the list. Not once have I heard a preacher call us to repent of racism, sexism, classism, nationalism, injustice, and indifference to the poor. What is deemed to be of immeasurable heavenly benefit can seem to be evidently of no earthly good for those among whom we live.

That brand of crucicentrism lays the foundation for the escapist apocalypticism embraced by millions of evangelicals. This hermeneutic promulgated a view of the future in which true believers in Jesus will be raptured from this evil world, stay with him in heaven for seven years, and then return with him to the earth to establish his millennial reign. According to this eschatological vision, the heavens and the earth we inhabit are "reserved unto fire against the day of judgment and perdition of ungodly men" (2 Pet. 3:7 KJV). Given this vision of the future and our revivalist view of the cross, many evangelicals reason that the only valid work for us on earth is to preach the gospel so that more people can escape the coming apocalypse. "Therefore," the reasoning goes, "since this world is going to be burned up in judgment and believers are going to be rescued from it, there's no reason to be involved in fighting injustice, poverty, violence, and the degradation of God's creation. God will take care of all that when he judges the world and destroys it with fire. We're going to heaven, and, while we're still here, we'll just preach the gospel and try to take as many others with us as possible." What a tragically impoverished understanding of the significance of the crucifixion of Jesus Christ.

Setting All Things Right

When Jesus died on the cross, everything changed. If we see the story of the Bible as cosmic history, and if we see the crucifixion of Jesus Christ as the climax of that history, and if we believe that the meaning of that history is found in the ultimate renewal of the cosmos under the reign of the risen Christ when he returns, then we dare not reduce the significance of the cross to just the personal forgiveness of sins and the promise of heaven. Jesus's final word before his last breath on the cross, "*tetelestai*" ("It is finished"; John 19:30), reverberates through the cosmos, disrupting and displacing Satan's rule. Through his death Jesus defeats sin, death, and evil; establishes his kingdom; and inaugurates his reign over all things in heaven and on earth (Matt. 28:19). As Miroslav Volf puts it, "The cross is not forgiveness pure and simple, but God's setting aright the world of injustice and deception."[5]

Revivalist religion privileges the simple over the complex and the tangible over the abstract. Forgiveness of sins, the alleviation of guilt, and the certainty of eternal life through the cross of Christ create a compelling offer, one to which untold millions have responded in the midst of a profound religious experience. It is the core message of the gospel proclaimed by evangelicals. Most would call it *the* gospel and appeal to Paul's affirmation of it in 1 Corinthians 15:3-5. "For what I received I passed on to you as of first importance: that Christ died for our sins according to the Scriptures, that he was buried, that he was raised on the third day according to the Scriptures, and that he appeared to Cephas, and then to the Twelve." This gospel of the cross remains central to our identity, and the next evangelicalism must build upon it to explore a more expansive view of what Jesus accomplished through the crucifixion.

The gospel we preach must never be less than "Christ died for our sins" (1 Cor. 15:3). But by itself, that affirmation can be used to construct an incomplete understanding of the way other New Testament authors use the Greek word (*euangelion*) translated "good news" and "gospel." For example, both Matthew and Mark use that word to describe the announcement that the kingdom of God is near (Mark 1:14–15; Matt. 4:23). That's really good news! Given the messianic expectation expressed in this language in the Greek translation of the prophetic literature of the Old Testament, it would be problematic to assume that Paul did not use that understanding to interpret the Messiah's (Christ's) death on the cross in passages like 1 Corinthians 15:3. Yet, because of our revivalist heritage and instincts, evangelicals have struggled mightily to rectify these two seemingly different uses of "gospel" in the New Testament—the gospel of the cross and the gospel of the kingdom of God. We're more comfortable with the personal, direct appeal of the gospel of the cross than the more theologically nuanced understanding that the gospel of the kingdom demands.

Theological education for the next evangelicalism must be grounded in this fuller, more robust articulation of crucicentrism, one that enfolds both the cross and the kingdom in our understanding of the gospel. Such an approach grounds our understanding of the gospel and our reading of the New Testament canonically in the great prophetic expectation in the Old Testament of the coming of Messiah. For example, in passages such as Isaiah 52:7, the one who brings "good news" (translated from Hebrew as *euangelion*, "gospel," in the LXX) proclaims that God's peace and salvation are at hand because the reign of God has begun. This understanding of gospel from the Old Testament, coupled with the first-century Greek understanding of gospel as the announcement of good news regarding military victories of the Roman Empire or the birth of a son to the emperor, undergirded the New Testament authors', including Paul's, use of *euangelion*. The gospel of the kingdom is the announcement that God's long-awaited kingdom and reign on the earth has come near. Through his miracles and teaching, Jesus's authority over demons, sin, death, disease, disability, classism, Pharisaism, racism, nationalism, and nature itself demonstrates that God is present in the world. His life foreshadows and announces that everything is changing because the kingdom is near.

There is no kingdom without the cross. The crucifixion establishes Jesus's reign over a kingdom unlike any earthly kingdom. It is the King, the Christ, who dies for our sins. Paul's gospel of the cross makes that perfectly clear (1 Cor. 15:3). Through his death, the fullness of life, both individual and communal, is made possible again. Through his seeming defeat, victory is won. The kingdom of God is unlike any earthly kingdom, but, make no mistake, it is earthly. Through the cross, the power of God wars against the dominion of sin, death, and evil on earth and defeats it. If the power of sin is broken when the crucified Jesus bears its penalty for everyone, death cannot have the final word. And if death cannot have the final word, evil will not ultimately prevail. That is the hope of the gospel. The resurrection vindicates and validates that hope. Everything is changed. The cosmos is set aright, and all of this matters as much on earth as it does in heaven.

But that deeper and richer understanding of the crucifixion and its implications for evangelical presence and engagement in the world hasn't been as widely adopted as the more individualistic offer of eternal salvation prominent in our revivalist heritage. That omission doesn't betray just a theological and hermeneutical problem. Our assignment of the efficacy of Jesus's death only to the spiritual realm lies more in Aristotelian and Enlightenment philosophical assumptions about cosmology and history than it does in biblical theology. These assumptions, many of which depart significantly from the cosmologies of the biblical authors, create a much greater separation between the spiritual and physical worlds than one can possibly find in Scripture. They influence our theology and hermeneutics far more pervasively than we know or care to admit. Like welding masks, they limit our ability to see clearly the cosmic scope of Christ's death on the cross in the heavenly and the earthly realms and its place in the biblical story.

A luxuriously rich and thick crucicentrism brings all the themes and threads of the biblical narrative together into one breathtaking cosmic event. Fleming Rutledge describes what happened that afternoon on the cross of Golgotha.

> All the manifold biblical images with their richness, complexity, and depth come together as one to say this: the righteousness of God is revealed in the cross of Christ. The "precious blood" of the Son of God is the perfect sacrifice for sin; the ransom is paid to deliver the captives; the gates of hell are stormed; the Red Sea is crossed and the enemy drowned; God's judgment has been executed upon Sin; the disobedience of Adam is recapitulated in the obedience of Christ; a new creation is coming into being; those who put their trust in Christ are incorporated into his life; the kingdoms of "the present evil age" are passing away and the promised kingdom of God is manifest not in triumphalist crusades, but in the cruciform witness of the church. From within "Adam's" (our) human flesh, the incarnate Son fought with and was victorious over Satan—on our behalf and in our place. Only this power, this transcendent victory won by the Son of God, is capable of reorienting the *kosmos* to its rightful Creator. This is what the righteousness of God has achieved through the cross and resurrection, is now accomplishing by the power of the Spirit, and will complete in the day of Christ Jesus.[6]

That's a gospel (*euangelion*) worth believing in and a gospel worth living for.

That's also a gospel worth dying for. And that dying is exactly what we who have believed the gospel are called to. We can never forget that the victory so beautifully and inspiringly described above came about through the brutal suffering, dehumanizing humiliation, and grotesque violence of the cross. If we are "in Christ," the humiliation of Christ and the suffering of Christ must be seen as essential and inevitable in the distinct way we are called to live out the hope of the gospel. Just as our life in Christ begins with the crucifixion, so our way of life in him must be cruciform. We will suffer "not the ordinary suffering that comes to everyone, but the particular affliction that must come to those who bear witness to the Lord's death. . . . The suffering endured by Christian witnesses does not come from a place of weakness, but from a place of strength."[7] The next evangelicalism must avoid the stunningly heretical view of the gospel that promises only prosperity and well-being. It's hard to imagine a more deceptive and destructive distortion of the gospel than that which prosperity preachers shill twenty-four hours a day worldwide on satellite television.

Jesus pulls no punches with his disciples. He tells them clearly, forcefully, and repeatedly that they must "take up their cross daily" and "lose their life" in order to follow him (Luke 9:23–24). If Jesus's death on the cross is the centerpiece of God's redemptive engagement in human history, it must take the same place in the lives of those who claim to know and worship him. Sacrifice, humility, love, and nonretaliation when reviled and humiliated—these are the characteristics of the one who refused to use his unrivaled power to defend himself and crush those who persecuted him. His cruciform death calls us to a cruciform life. It calls us to love our enemies and pray for those who persecute us (Matt. 5:44); to turn the other cheek when assaulted by an evil person (Matt. 5:38–39); to bless, not curse, those who persecute us (Rom. 12:14); to step away from revenge (Rom. 12:19); and not to retaliate when insulted and degraded (1 Pet. 2:23). The cruciform life demands full trust in the wisdom, goodness, and power of God (1 Pet. 2:21–23). It is the life that we who claim the cross as our salvation are called to pursue. We cannot be known as the people of the gospel if we are unwilling to follow Jesus in the way of the cross.

Cruciformity assaults the values of every earthly kingdom. Victory through defeat, life through death, joy through suffering, riches through poverty, satisfaction through denial—all these reversals are counterintuitive, if not plain foolish in the eyes of the world. Yet, the cross demands them of those who dare to testify to belief in the crucified Son of God. Cruciformity is the only solution to the evangelical maladies of "Jesus machismo," celebrityism, and prosperity theology.

The centrality of crucicentrism and the call to cruciformity create the single most difficult formational challenge in evangelical theological education. If the crucifixion is the center of the biblical story, the nexus of God's redemptive engagement in human history, the decisive defeat of Satan's reign, and the foundation of Christian hope, then it must occupy the center of the theological curriculum, the axial theme upon which all academic disciplines find their place in our programming. In the crucifixion we see the character, person, and work of God most clearly. In the crucifixion we see the heights and depths of the human condition in ways seen nowhere else in Scripture. And in the crucifixion we see in bold relief our mission as God's people. To put it another way, if the student cannot find his or her way to the cross in every class in an evangelical seminary, we have lost our way as evangelical theological educators. *Crux sola est nostra theologia.*

If cruciformity is the way of the cross, then it must become the ultimate formational outcome toward which we journey together in theological education. Values work is deep work, slow work, painful work. The values of the cross emerge in the crucibles of suffering, failure, confusion, and loss through starkly honest reflection and baldly sacrificial acts of mercy shared in relationships of trust. Such relationships gain traction and depth through shared experience. They can lead to redemption but, like the cross, only through pain and suffering. Whereas meaningful, redemptive, personal relationships cannot be contrived through structured learning experiences, they can be nurtured in them. Theological education that points toward cruciformity must create opportunities for learners to go to places they would not naturally go personally, experientially, relationally, and missionally in order to lose themselves in the gospel for the sake of the world. And it must provide safe places for the kind of honest reflection within a community of fellow Jesus followers that helps forge and refine the values of the cross in the lives of students and faculty. The next evangelicalism can carve out a distinct identity only through cruciformity, a way of life that has nothing in common with the thirst for political power and victory in the culture wars that our movement has become known for.

Because of its historical, theological, biblical, and ethical significance, the cross must take center place not only in the songs of our movement but also in our lives, our churches, and our schools. *It must define us more than any other truth and shape us more than any other value.* The task of theological education for the next evangelicalism is to guide the movement into a broader and deeper crucicentrism. God knows, we desperately need it. And the world desperately needs it as well, even if they don't know it.

9

Conversion

The son of a moonshiner and an alcoholic in his own right, my grandpa found out quickly that his new wife wouldn't put up with his drinking. Returning to their house drunk one Saturday afternoon, he was met on the back porch with a very persuasive cast-iron skillet, a bucket of cold water, and two pronouncements: he'd better never show up at their house drunk again, and he would be with his wife in church the next morning. As family lore narrates it, Grandpa got saved that Sunday morning and never had another drop of alcohol. All I know is this: my grandpa was a godly, respected, generous, honest, hardworking man who served as a deacon in our hometown Baptist church. His changed life changed the trajectory of a family on a path of self-destruction. He died sitting in his spot on the settee in the family room with his Bible open in his lap. I still have that Bible.

Every evangelical, it seems, has a conversion story, the more dramatic, the better. As revivalist religion, evangelicalism sees these stories as proof that the gospel message is indeed "the power of God that brings salvation to everyone who believes" (Rom. 1:16).

The lyrics of "Amazing Grace" capture the essence of our view of conversionism:

> Amazing grace! how sweet the sound,
> That saved a wretch like me!
> I once was lost but now am found;
> Was blind but now I see.[1]

We love that hymn. It pretty much sums up what we believe about our relationship with God. We are sinners, "wretches" before a holy God and unable to do anything to change our life and our eternal destiny. But God pours out his amazing grace on us. And when he does that, our life is changed forever. From lost to found and from blind to seeing, God changes us and brings us into a personal relationship with him. That hymn strikes deep chords of gratitude in the hearts of evangelicals, and a deep love for the God who would do that for us. Of the four priorities we've identified in evangelicalism's theological DNA, conversionism is the most personally experienced and deeply cherished throughout the movement. There is no evangelicalism without a strong belief that God changes lives.

Even those who grow up attending a local church and participating in the life of that church often feel the need to have some kind of personal conversion story. The unspoken evangelical rule is that everyone should be able to testify to a personal decision to follow Jesus. The more details you can recite about the moment of conversion, the better. If you grew up in an evangelical church, you often talk about "asking Jesus into your heart" at a young age; or you speak of "rededicating your life to Christ" as a teen or young adult. Both of these kinds of stories count in building evangelical street cred, but not quite as much as a titillating story of deliverance from a life of perdition and reckless excess. We might be inclined to chuckle at ourselves when reading that last sentence, but the point remains: evangelicals believe that lives need to be changed, and God does that through faith in Jesus Christ.

Conversionism is the essence of revivalist religion. With Jonathan Edwards painting graphic images of sinners in the hands of an angry God and George Whitefield warning sinners that they dare not delay putting their faith in Christ because they may not live to see another day, the necessity and urgency of conversion becomes the core message of revivalist preaching. Conversion is typically understood as immediate and personal. Each individual must believe in the gospel, and, at the moment of belief, that individual's life is transformed. Bearing the long theological tail of the Reformation's decoupling of salvation from the mediation of the Roman Catholic Church and magnified through the enduring influence of our revivalist heritage, many evangelicals today see no essential theological role for the church in the conversion of the individual.

Nor does our vision of convertive piety[2] necessarily include the contribution of, or even participation in, a local church. Many evangelicals seem to be comfortable with the idea of a "churchless" salvation and spiritual life. And why not? If salvation is a siloed transaction between an individual and God for the purpose of having our sins forgiven and being assured of an afterlife in heaven, then life after conversion must also be an individual, personal relationship with the one who forgave our sins and ensured our eternity in heaven. Of course, the harsh reality is that we keep on sinning after our conversion, and many of the problems we experienced before conversion linger on in our lives. That's why for many evangelicals, postconversion life can become little more than a daily exercise in sin management and the quest for God's intervention in the problems we experience. In many ways, evangelicalism today is as obsessed with sin management as the medieval Catholicism that the Reformers rejected.

Conversionism assumes that we are deeply aware of our own sins and acknowledge our need to call out to Christ for forgiveness. Again, our revivalist roots loom large in contemporary evangelical practice here. The sins we are called to acknowledge before God are almost exclusively personal, moral failings. Our participation in broader cultural sins like racism, economic injustice, and misogyny typically remains unnamed and unrepented. An individualistic approach to conversion simply cannot address the culturally acceptable "sins" by which most of us live. That's why many evangelicals could testify to saving faith in Christ while justifying slavery, enforcing Jim Crow laws, defending racial segregation, and assuming patriarchy as the normative paradigm for gendered social relationships. Although we would like to think our hermeneutical practice, theological acumen, and moral sensibilities are more sophisticated today, we still live too comfortably with ways of thinking, valuing, and behaving that contradict the ways of the kingdom. And that will likely always be the case as long as we see conversion merely as a spiritual transaction between us sinners and God. We need a far more theologically robust and missionally framed view of conversion.

Conversionism also allows us to separate our salvation experience from our sense of national identity, civic responsibility, and our approach to political engagement. If conversion is just a spiritual transaction between an individual and God, how we engage in politics, for example, doesn't fall under its purview. The way evangelicals have understood, articulated, and practiced conversionism, therefore, has been a significant contributor to our current identity crisis. It has allowed us to prioritize and engage the political process with little significant theological understanding of how our conversion creates and prioritizes a new communal identity that forms the foundation for cultural presence and engagement. Addressing this oversight is a critical task for evangelical theological education moving forward. Alongside a more expansive understanding of the death of Christ on the cross, theological education for the next evangelicalism must develop a more expansive vision of gospel identity and mission as the necessary outcomes of conversion.

Far more than just a siloed spiritual transaction between a repentant sinner and God that punches one's ticket to heaven, conversion brings heaven to earth. It creates a new identity for those who believe in Christ and ushers them into a community whose purpose is to be the presence of God on earth until King Jesus returns. This new community is commissioned and empowered by the Holy Spirit to bring shalom, the fullness of life, to all who encounter it. When we put our faith in the finished work of Christ on the cross, we become a part of the community called to embody the kingdom of God on earth for the sake of the world. This vision of the significance of conversion expands and enriches the typical "ticket to heaven" approach of evangelical conversionism. In fact, it eclipses that understanding with a vision of life and mission on earth that the traditional view can never achieve.

The People of God

"Dad, who am I? Am I an American? Am I a Pole?"[3] When your twelve-year-old son asks a heartfelt question, you pay attention.

We were flying from Wrocław, Poland, where we had previously lived for seven years, to Warsaw to catch a flight back to the United States. It had been a year since we'd moved from our home in Poland to live and work in the States. In his twelve years of life, our son had lived in seven different houses in five different cities, and in three different countries on two continents. That tally doesn't include numerous nights spent in hotels and in friends' and family members' homes. During the seven years we had lived in Poland, he had learned to speak Polish fluently, often being mistaken for a native speaker, and had built a tight network of Polish friends through the local elementary school that he attended. All of our close relationships were with Poles.

Leaving Poland the year before had been a physically and emotionally draining experience for all of us. And our first year living in the United States had been the most difficult of our lives. We felt like immigrants living in a country not our own. But we buckled down and entered into life in the suburbs of a major city. Life felt frenzied in the United States: schools, driving, work, driving, shopping, driving, sports, driving, church, driving. To us, the United States was a foreign country with a way of life and a set of cultural values that we didn't particularly understand and definitely didn't like.

That's why we jumped at the chance for him to return with me to Poland for a couple of weeks almost exactly one year after we'd left the place we considered home. I'll never forget the scene when we landed at the airport in our city. Just beyond the chain-link fence around the perimeter of the tarmac stood several of his former classmates waving and yelling to him as we got off the plane. Once we cleared customs, the real fun began. He switched into Polish seamlessly, and the parents of one of his closest friends gathered him up, put him in their car, and drove him home. I didn't see him for the next two weeks, as the families of his school friends passed him from one home to another. We reconnected at the airport and walked to the plane with the same group of kids behind the fence waving and shouting their good-byes.

Leaving that place a second time stung even more deeply than our departure the year before. His tearful "Dad, who am I?" came from a heart that was hurting. He felt uprooted, displaced, and disoriented, somehow cast adrift in questions of identity, relationships, and place. Our whole family did. I answered instinctively with the only thing that seemed permanent in my life.

"Son, you are a child of God."[4]

We all bear multiple identities—family, nationality, gender, race, profession, social class—and all of them matter. They form our sense of self and function socially to create ingroup-outgroup dynamics. Our identities spur us to build relationships with some and to separate from others; they create both comfort and discomfort, and far too many other polarities in our lives. All of our identities matter; being the people of God matters most.

Followers of Christ have an identity that overlays all other identities. The apostle Paul says it this way, "So in Christ Jesus you are all children of God through faith, for all of you who were baptized into Christ have clothed yourselves with Christ. There is neither Jew nor Gentile, neither slave nor free, nor is there male and female, for you are all one in Christ Jesus" (Gal. 3:26–28). We who have put our faith in Christ are the people of God before we are anything else. Before our nationality, ethnicity, gender, occupation, even family, we find our primary identity in our relationship with Christ and his people, an identity that must never be supplanted or subverted.

As jarring as it may sound to the heirs of revivalist conversionism, our primary identity is communal, not individual. We collectively as the people of God are adopted, grafted in, welcomed, and embraced. Grounded in the vision of the kingdom of God established by the death and resurrection of Jesus, our identity is both cosmic and earthly, spiritual and physical. As the people of God, we experience his presence with our hands lifted high in praise and with our arms embracing the broken and rejected of the world.

We are God's presence in the world. A community living out his presence will, by necessity, celebrate diverse peoples and be shaped by diverse voices. Just as the God we worship is three distinct persons living in perfect union as one God, so too as God's people we must represent unity and distinction. As God's people, the diversity that frequently inhibits meaningful relationships in the broader society should become a source of deeply satisfying and enriching relationships in our faith communities. The unity of God's people foreshadows the purpose of God "to bring unity to all things in heaven and on earth under Christ" (Eph. 1:10b). Both a lack of unity and a lack of diversity in our churches contradict the reconciling work of Christ and mar our testimony of the power of redemption in a world riven by sectarian, ethnic, racial, and political hostilities.

Diverse voices in the community provide an opportunity to expose those deeply embedded culturally validated sins that cannot be discerned in the echo chamber of a monocultural, racially segregated, patriarchal, and sociologically homogenous community. We often think that racism creates segregation, but it's also true that segregation fosters racism.[5] In like manner, theological differences in evangelicalism may be less the cause and more the effect of strict, strident, separatist, and segregated fundamentalism masquerading as evangelicalism. How confusing to the world is it when the community of faith fractures because of partisan politics, egotistical rivalries, and doctrinal squabbles over issues of secondary importance? Disunity of any kind in the church is "an intolerable anomaly" and "a violent contradiction of its own fundamental nature. His [Christ's] reconciling work is one, and we cannot be His ambassadors reconciling the world to God, if we have not ourselves been willing to be reconciled to one another."[6]

A Richer Conversionism

In order for us to live out our identity as the people of God, theological education for the next evangelicalism must prioritize in its curriculum a theologically richer, thicker understanding of conversion that is grounded in a truly crucicentric ecclesiology. It must broaden and deepen the movement's understanding of what it means to be the people of God. That will be no small feat. Baptist theologian Millard Erickson has written, "At no point in the history of Christian thought has the doctrine of the church received the direct and complete attention which other doctrines have received."[7] Although overcooked with the use of the qualifier "Christian," when speaking of evangelical theology and history, Erickson's quote sadly rings true.

The transdenominational character of evangelicalism challenges the idea that there might even be an evangelical ecclesiology. One theologian asked in the title of his chapter in the edited volume *Evangelical Ecclesiology: Reality or Illusion?*, "Is Evangelical Ecclesiology an Oxymoron?"[8] Indeed, traditional approaches to ecclesiology in the theological academy have focused on the areas of disagreement between traditions and denominations more than the common commitments that ought to be characteristic of the whole church. When ecclesiology becomes little more than a debate over differences in sacraments, ordinances, polity, structures, and practices, its perceived irrelevance overwhelms its genuine significance.

Unfortunately, our revivalist, individualistic understanding of the gospel and conversion relegates ecclesiology to a place of secondary importance in the theological curriculum. If the church is not an essential part of salvation and convertive piety, why elevate ecclesiology to a position of prominence in theological studies? Even our biblicism has added to the diminished place of ecclesiology in our schools. With our tendency to absolutize certain, but not all, of the behaviors of the emerging communities of faith during the New Testament era rather than engage in a canonically nuanced and contextualized theological reflection on what it means to live out the authority of all Scripture as the people of God's mission in the world, we use ecclesiology to divide the church at the expense of our mission. The consequences of an underdeveloped ecclesiology are severe. A limited vision of our identity as the people of God has exacerbated the degradation of our identity and witness. It's no wonder that evangelicalism has become little more than a political bloc in the public square. Because we haven't developed an expansive, beautiful, and inspiring vision of our identity and significance for the world as the gathered people of God, we march with conviction toward being far less than we were created to be.

Theological education for the next evangelicalism must prosecute an ecclesiology grounded in the story of the Bible as universal history with the cross as its inflection point and the consummation of God's redemptive mission as the source of history's ultimate meaning. Undergirding the entire story is God's beneficent desire to be known and worshiped by all peoples so that they may find the fullness of life in him. The realization of that desire is God's mission, and for reasons never fully explained in Scripture, God has entrusted the prosecution of his redemptive mission in the world to his people. We are the people of God's mission; that's our primary identity, the lens through which all other personal and social identities must be viewed. The significance of conversion is found in the incorporation of those who believe in Christ into a new humanity, a new community, the very presence of God in the world.

Since the end of history is already revealed in the grand climax of the biblical narrative, that eschatological vision grounds and animates the church. The redeemed have already tasted the salvation to come, the great consummation of redemption when everything that's wrong in the world will be made right, everything that's broken in the world will be made whole, and everything that's ugly in the world will be made beautiful. Humanity longs for a world with perfect justice, the fullness of life, and beauty beyond our most vivid imagination. And the people of God have already tasted what a world like that will mean. Even more, through the indwelling presence of the Holy Spirit, God's people pursue the justice, reconciliation, and shalom of God's new creation in the midst of brokenness, alienation, and death. Our privilege is to offer a foretaste of the future and point the world to the only One who can bring it to pass. Lesslie Newbigin describes the church as a sign "that points people to a reality beyond what we can see."[9] The world longs for what the church is created to embody, the certain hope of redemption.

Theological education for the sake of the world frames ecclesiology with the world's longing. Unwilling to be trapped in the endless ecclesiological disputes between different theological traditions and denominations, such an ecclesiology embraces the radical truth that the church does not live for itself. It exists to be the hope of the gospel for the world. The church is a public body, not a private, sectarian gathering just for the benefit of its members. The church, self-titled as *ekklēsia*, "is the public assembly of God . . . the new humanity called into the end-time kingdom by God and launched into the public life of the Roman Empire to challenge all competing allegiances. . . . It is a public body that must manifest the comprehensive and restorative salvation of the kingdom."[10]

The church doesn't just *do* public theology; it *is* public theology. The people of God make manifest to the world the redemptive power of gospel. That's not just what we do, it's who we are. Unfortunately, because our theologically impoverished conversionism leads to a diminished vision of the people of God, evangelicalism has adopted an identity scathingly critiqued by the prophets in the Old Testament and inimical to God's engagement in human history: an embattled and aggrieved minority called to wage war against the culture through a naked grab for political power using the tactics, values, and ethics of every other voting bloc. As Israel and Judah adopted the gods and practices of neighboring peoples, they surrendered their identity and privilege to be the presence of the one true God for the sake of the nations.

And we've done the same. We, too, have abandoned our privilege to be the very presence of God, the embodiment of the gospel of Jesus Christ. Created to be a contrast people, we've blurred the lines that would distinguish us as a unique, life-giving presence in society. Our mission, our *raison d'être*, is to point people to Jesus and the hope of redemption. But we've decided to pursue something far less important and far less magnificent than being his presence on the earth. Unless we admit to ourselves that in the broader culture we have become nothing more than a conservative political bloc using religious language and allegiance to pursue the same ends as all other political blocs, we will continue to be far less than we are created to be. To the degree that we are known primarily by anything other than the gospel of Jesus Christ, our idolatries are revealed.

Theological education for the next evangelicalism must enrich and thicken the movement's understanding of conversion by placing it in the framework of a more expansive view of the cross and a renewed ecclesiology. Rather than just a personal transaction between God and the individual, conversion ushers us into a new identity as the people of God and a new sense of purpose in the mission of God. That new identity and calling, grounded in the biblical narrative through the death of Christ on the cross, turn the believing community outward toward a world longing for the redemption we have already foreseen and tasted.

In like manner, theological education must be turned outward. Theological education for the sake of the world answers the world's questions, not just the endlessly disputed questions of competing theological systems. We've spent far too long talking to ourselves about matters that only matter to us, creating self-justifying echo chambers that only heed "safe" voices, those with whom we already agree. If we're honest with ourselves, the world's posture toward evangelical theological education isn't one of hostility, it's indifference. We don't matter to the world because, to our shame, the world doesn't matter to us.

Theological education for the next evangelicalism must see its mission as helping shape God's people to engage the questions, doubts, and needs of the world with the redemptive power of the gospel and the life-changing truth of Scripture. Intellectually honest, courageously curious, and compellingly compassionate—these should be the traits of an evangelical theological education for the sake of the world. In conversation with the world—listening, reflecting, learning—we find our faith strengthened, not threatened; our theology enriched, not eroded; and our testimony emboldened, not cowed. That kind of theological education will require the traditional academic disciplines to broaden and diversify the voices students hear. We must be quick to acknowledge, however, that such an approach will put some schools at risk in those denominations where the defaming ire of those who still voice the posture of our fundamentalist heritage and who fear engagement with those outside the community of faith can do real damage to an institution. The fear of being labeled "liberal" in evangelical theological schools cuts deeply into our collective psyche.

Mission is messy. Our privilege and calling as the people of God are to step into the mess with the message of redemption. Theological education built upon the hope of the gospel for the sake of the world can help the next evangelicalism take that step.

Mission

Involvement in a campus ministry during college so powerfully and meaningfully transformed me that I wanted to tell everyone I knew what Christ had done for me. That seemed like the natural thing to do. The leaders in that campus ministry emphasized that telling others about Christ is a core expression of our faith. They provided training and materials for us to use when "sharing Christ" with our friends. We prayed for those who didn't know Christ. We invited them to gatherings. We built relationships with them through playing sports, studying together, and just hanging out. None of this was done with nefarious intent. We weren't trying to recruit or manipulate people into joining a controlling sect. We talked with others about our own faith in Christ because it meant so much to us and we wanted them to experience what we had experienced. And several of my friends and acquaintances put their faith in Christ. Those early years of renewed faith changed the course of my life.

Most evangelicals believe they should share their faith with others whenever the opportunity to do so presents itself. So, as appropriate, many of us naturally and humbly tell others what Christ has done for us and what he can do for them. In a pluralistic and secular society, that sentiment may sound extreme and arrogant, if not just plain naïve, to those outside the movement. We must not allow the resilience of our conviction that Jesus offers grace and mercy to all to be overwhelmed by the stifling indifference of many and the outright hostility of some toward the presence and engagement of the faith community in society, especially when that engagement involves making the gospel known outside the walls of local churches. The stereotype of angry, dogmatic, judgmental evangelicals shouting condemnation and predicting doom for those who do not believe plays well in the press but doesn't match the experience of millions of believers. Most of us engage those around us out of compassion and an honest concern to help meet whatever needs we can. Evangelicals simply believe that their faith ought to be seen and heard by those who know them. There can be no expression of evangelicalism that does not include an instinctive impulse to help others find the fullness of life in Christ.

It is that outward expression of our faith that David Bebbington points to when identifying activism as an enduring priority in evangelicalism. He defines evangelical activism as "the expression of the gospel in effort."[1] From the time of the great revivals in the colonial era, evangelicalism made its presence seen, heard, and felt in ways that no other religious group had. Its transdenominational and transregional character allowed the movement to expand through evangelistic crusades without the traditional physical limitations of institutional religion. These crusades expressed the most widely held understanding of activism among evangelicals—the proclamation of the gospel, the saving work of Christ on the cross, to as many people as possible.

Evangelical activism after the Civil War created another wave of widespread revivals and an ongoing commitment to meaningful social engagement through meeting the needs of the poor and the powerless in urban, rural, and frontier settings. It also included institution building. Whether on the ever-expanding western frontier or in the demographically changing urban centers in the East and Upper Midwest, evangelicals built and staffed schools, universities, hospitals, churches, orphanages, and soup kitchens. Through these endeavors, evangelicals gave "expression of the gospel in effort" in frontier towns where it was not already present and in cities where people's physical needs were not being met by local governments. The impulse to make our faith known to others through both word and deed springs from a place of deep conviction and compassion.

These "expressions of the gospel in effort" contributed to the widespread respect that evangelicals enjoyed in many areas. As noted earlier, however, we must acknowledge that many evangelical churches, denominations, and individuals continued to uphold the assumptions—white supremacy, patriarchy, classism—and the legal structures and broadly accepted practices that perpetuated social injustice, including denying emancipated slaves and women the right to own property, vote, and attend school. Evangelical activism in some areas supported the attitudes and practices of white supremacy while in other areas it worked to overturn them. These same inconsistencies were seen in the areas of women's rights and the protection of workers' rights. Although engaged in helping the working poor meet their basic physical needs, many evangelicals opposed the development of trade unions and legislation to combat the unfair labor practices that plagued much of the working class in America since the nation's inception. Unfortunately, the common theological commitments of evangelicalism do not always eventuate in common goals, priorities, and practices in our activism.

Lacking a robust theology of the cosmic, ecclesiological, and missional implications of crucicentrism and conversionism, some evangelicals have struggled to develop an activism that equally values evangelism and social engagement. That struggle has exacerbated our inability to develop a coherent and meaningful approach to our presence and engagement in the public square, a failing painfully obvious in our current crisis of identity and mission.

As a movement, we seem to like binary approaches to just about everything. Activism means either evangelism or social engagement. That deficiency has perpetuated the absurd ongoing debate about the primacy of one expression of our activism over the other, with both sides accusing each other of propagating an "unbiblical" view of the gospel. It is no small irony that the architects of our current identity crisis held fast to evangelism as the biblical "expression of the gospel in effort" while urging evangelicals to a political activism with the language of "culture wars" that effectively undermined our testimony in our evangelistic efforts. Evangelicals have been calling sinners to repent and find forgiveness for their sins in the shed blood of Jesus while waging war against these "sinners" in the political and cultural arenas. Through far-reaching media empires, some have shifted the public perception of evangelical presence in society from Billy Graham's offer of peace with God because of the love of Jesus Christ shown in his death on the cross to nothing more than strident condemnation of liberals, feminists, members of the LGBTQ+ communities, Democrats, and just about everyone else who isn't a conservative Republican.

Political activism without theological grounding in the gospel has no clear goal other than to defeat political opponents, a nihilism that is inimical to the biblical narrative and the gospel we claim to believe. At the same time, preaching a gospel of mercy and grace without being the presence of mercy and grace through compassionately meeting physical and social needs in our communities strips our gospel message in the minds of many of both credibility and relevance.

Ought our approach to activism preclude political engagement? Not at all. What it does preclude, however, is uncritical, partisan political engagement for any purpose other than to point the world to the risen Christ through our actions and to raise a prophetic voice for social change grounded in the virtues and values of the kingdom of God. Our current identity crisis stems from political activism that uncritically supports candidates and policies that contradict those very kingdom virtues and values. We are driven more by outrage whipped up by fearmongering than by a righteous yearning for the shalom of the kingdom and compassion for those who do not know Jesus. The association of our movement with Christian nationalism and white supremacy through our uncritical support for Donald Trump, frequently masked with misquoted phrases and verses from the Bible, makes our current political activism even more damaging to our identity and witness. The activism of the next evangelicalism, including engagement in the political process, must chart a different path, take a different tone, and pursue a different end. Only then can we begin to live out the hope of the gospel in credible and compelling ways.

The language of activism may itself contribute to our unfortunate compartmentalization of evangelism and social engagement. Henri J. M. Nouwen, Donald P. McNeill, and Douglas A. Morrison draw a helpful distinction between *impatient activism* and *patient action*. Patient action requires an enduring presence that seeks the good of others, sometimes with few tangible results. Our society, however, values success over presence, a bias that lends itself to impatient activism in search of immediate results. "In our society, which equates worth with productivity, patient action is very difficult. We tend to be so concerned with doing something worthwhile, bringing about changes, planning, organizing, structuring and restructuring that we often seem to forget that it is not we who redeem, but God."[2] Our revivalist heritage lends itself to an activism that yields immediate, tangible results. It's easy to count the number of converts at a revival meeting and the number of votes cast for political candidates; it's far more difficult to measure the steady, long-term transformation of lives and communities through compassionate, long-suffering, enduring presence.

Add to our idols of productivity and efficiency the gods of "new" and "better," and we find ourselves in frenzied pursuit of a satisfaction that always lies just beyond our reach. We are seduced into believing that we have the power to create change that only God can bring about. Evangelicals have drunk deeply from the tankard of success. And it tastes really good. So we pursue success with an impatience born of arrogance and an addiction to "more." No one has to convince most evangelical ministry leaders to do more, to seek more, to reap more. We mistakenly think that's how we can know God is blessing us. One would be hard pressed to identify a religious group in the United States that is more entrepreneurial, more driven by the pursuit of bigger and better, more frequently entrapped by the shortsighted folly of "ends justifying means" strategies, and more prone to spectacular failures of leadership than evangelicalism. We've fallen prey to a religious celebrityism that elevates those whose blogs have more readers, whose tweets garner more re-tweets, whose books sell more copies, whose broadcasts reach more consumers, whose concerts fill more arenas, and whose sermons pack more pews. And it all seems to fit our oft-denied but patently evident evangelical conviction that more activity pleases God more.

Impatient activism seems like the only reasonable response when we've convinced ourselves that those who oppose us have far more power than they actually do. The battle cry "We're at war!" raises our pulse and opens our purse. Having taken on the identity of an aggrieved and embattled minority, we foment urgency to act to protect ourselves. What a tragedy. I will not soon forget a friend saying with sincere conviction during the 2016 presidential campaign, "If Hillary Clinton wins the election, Denver Seminary is doomed." Dog-whistle issues like the loss of religious freedom create the fear and anger needed to keep the faithful reaching for their wallets and rallying to the indignation *du jour*.

Contemporary evangelical activism differs little from the activism of other social and political movements. But that's not the activism Jesus calls us to. "The disciples speak of their actions as manifestations of God's active presence. They act not to prove their power, but to show God's power; they act not to redeem people but to reveal God's redemptive grace; they act not to create a new world, but to open hearts and ears to the one who sits on the throne and says, 'Now I am making the whole creation new' (Rev 21:5)."[3] At the end of the day, we need to ask ourselves one simple question about our activism: "Does it draw more attention to us or to Jesus?"

Patient action, faithful presence, steadfast endurance, and costly compassion may not be sexy enough to fit the mold of success in our culture, but they are exactly what we are called to as the people of God. The next evangelicalism must embrace its identity as a foretaste of the kingdom, an embodied presence of the new humanity and the new life that faith in the redemptive power of the gospel brings. Lesslie Newbigin states this beautifully: "The chief contribution of the Church to the renewing of the social order is to be itself a new social order."[4] In a pluralistic society we can shout the words of the gospel, but we cannot outshout the myriad other voices clamoring for the attention of an anxious and distracted populace. We've tried that approach for the last fifty years, and our voice is thinner, shriller, and less convincing today than it's ever been. An uncompromised and unabashedly Jesus-centered, compassion-driven, self-sacrificing, mercy-filled, and grace-soaked presence of the people of God is the only way the gospel can gain a hearing in our world. That kind of presence only comes about through patient action. Asks Newbigin, "How is it possible that the gospel should be credible, that people should come to believe that the power which has the last word in human affairs is represented by a man hanging on a cross? I am suggesting that the only answer, the only hermeneutic of the gospel, is a congregation of men and women who believe it and live by it."[5] The hope of the gospel, the restoration of all things, embraces all of life. That's why we must embody it in all of life to be a credible witness of it to all who know us.

Theological education for the next evangelicalism must be organized around a vision of the mission of the church that supersedes the expressions of evangelical activism that have led to our current identity crisis. That vision must be local and global, wholeheartedly embracing both word and deed as essential gospel witness. Its curricular focus must be the spiritual, intellectual, and relational formation of those whose beliefs, virtues, values, and practices embody the gospel in the public square through patient action.

Pushing beyond the disciplinary boundaries that serve the academic guilds better than the broader people of God, theological education for the next evangelicalism must integrate into every discrete curricular unit theological, hermeneutical, missiological, and formational learning outcomes built around the question, "How can the people of God live out their identity as a sign pointing the world to the gospel of the risen Christ and his kingdom?"

To address that question, some oft-neglected areas of instruction must take a more prominent place in the curricular emphases of theological education programs: the Spirit's presence and empowerment of God's people, cultural exegesis and contextualized witness, and the global mandate of Jesus. In many evangelical seminaries these emphases receive but a passing comment or a couple of lectures in an entire degree program. But that is hardly sufficient if we are to change theological training to shape and serve the next evangelicalism as the presence of the hope of the gospel in this world.

"Who's Afraid of the Holy Spirit? The Uneasy Conscience of a Non-Charismatic Evangelical"[6] is the provocative title of an address given by New Testament professor Daniel B. Wallace at a regional meeting of the Evangelical Theological Society (ETS). I assume that hardly any of the attendees raised a hand and said, "I am," in response to Professor Wallace's question. But many probably should have. Given the typical makeup of an ETS gathering in that region at that time, most attendees probably came from noncharismatic, predominately white graduate schools where the abiding presence and empowerment of the Holy Spirit are not regularly incorporated into the formational process. Although they may not admit to being afraid of the Holy Spirit, many pursue their calling as scholars and faculty members as if they are. Such would also be the case in most ATS-accredited schools. If we are honest with ourselves, we need to admit that in most evangelical theological education we just don't know what to do with the Holy Spirit except make him an abstract object of study.

Most of the angst and disagreement about the presence and empowerment of the Holy Spirit in evangelicalism come from two groups: those who believe that the so-called sign gifts—speaking in tongues, healing, and prophesying (among others)—are essential marks of someone experiencing the Spirit's presence, and those who believe such gifts ceased to be operative in the church at the end of the apostolic age. Although both views are not widely held in evangelical seminaries, they frame the conversation and the practices of many schools.

When the framework for considering the presence and empowerment of the Spirit in the life of the believer is an all-or-nothing choice between the two marginal views, we miss the critical truth that the Spirit's presence and empowerment are the *only way* God's people can live out their identity and pursue their mission. The absence of profound and regular experiences of the presence and empowerment of the Holy Spirit in theological education undermines the academy's ability to discern God's truth and will. And, thereby, the most powerful way God shapes his people to fulfill their calling is excluded.

It is the Spirit's presence and power in the people of God that point the world to Jesus. Such was the promise the resurrected Jesus gave to the disciples just before he ascended to the right hand of the Father in heaven (Acts 1:8). We dare not forget that the Spirit's primary ministry is to testify to the Son. He accomplishes God's mission in the world; it's his mission, not ours.

> As the church reaches out to meet the world's needs, the Spirit witnesses to the coming kingdom. As the church does deeds of justice, mercy, compassion, and shalom, the Spirit witnesses in and through those deeds to the kingdom come in Jesus. As the church becomes deeply and lovingly involved in the sorrow and misery of the world, the Spirit points to Christ and his rule. . . . Where the power of the Spirit is at work producing new life and deeds of justice, questions about this new reality will open opportunities for a verbal witness. In these words the Spirit witnesses to Christ.[7]

If it is through the Spirit that God empowers his people to prosecute his mission in the world, theological education for the sake of the world must intentionally create space for the work of the Spirit in our pedagogy and our community.

Can theological education for the next evangelicalism foster an abiding experience of the Spirit's presence and empowerment? Yes, but only if we are willing to admit that there is an enduring legacy of the depersonalization and objectification of God in many evangelical theological schools, and only if we intentionally nourish the more personal, more experiential, more emotional dimensions of learning. The quest to *understand* God's person and ways, although right and good, must never overwhelm our desire to *believe*, to *love*, and to *worship* our God. Further, in order to experience the Spirit's transformative presence, we must recover the centrality of community in theological education. Through communal worship, communal prayer, communal wrestling with the hard questions, and communal mission, we experience the presence and power of the Spirit of God together. And the community must hear diverse Scripture-drenched, theologically informed, Spirit-emboldened voices— black and white voices, female and male voices, Hispanic voices, Asian voices, indigenous voices—all hungering and thirsting for the righteousness of the kingdom through the presence and empowerment of the Spirit, all naming Jesus as the King of kings and Lord of lords. That's the kind of theological education that can help carve out the next evangelicalism and create a compelling testimony of the hope of the gospel in our world.

For the next evangelicalism, we need to turn theological education inside out. If the purpose of our endeavor is the formation of communities living out a credible and compelling testimony of the Son in a world that wonders why he matters, we have to know that world and love that world. In this sense, we can say that evangelical theological education needs to be more worldly.

As described above, my faith came alive in college when I realized that God could use me to point others to Jesus. And that's why I spent my college years loving, engaging, and spending time with people who did not know Jesus, while praying that I might have an opportunity to tell them about my faith in Christ. But when I started seminary, people who didn't know Jesus didn't seem to matter to my fellow students or the faculty. We didn't talk about them, except to condemn them and their way of life. We didn't honestly consider their questions and objections to our faith, except to refute them. We didn't pray for them, we didn't grieve for them, we didn't try to understand them, and we didn't build relationships with them. It was as if they didn't exist to us and we didn't exist for them. Our focus was inward, and our primary concerns were exegetical accuracy, theological orthodoxy, and everyone else's errors and sins. Ministry-oriented classes focused on techniques for preaching, teaching, and leading other believers in local churches. Basically, my seminary experience could be described as Christians helping Christians learn how to help Christians be better Christians. Nowhere did the world fit into that equation. Theological education for the next evangelicalism must help students develop as much skill exegeting culture as interpreting Scripture. We cannot create a credible and compelling presence of the gospel among those we do not know. And we will not do it among those we do not love.

At some point, we have to answer the question, "Who ultimately should experience the benefit of theological education?" Theological educators tend to answer that question in different ways. Some strive to make their primary contribution through their scholarship. Their energy and gifts are focused on contributions to the body of knowledge in their field of expertise. These theological educators locate their efforts—publishing, presenting papers, overseeing research projects—in the academy and its attendant gatherings, entities, networks, and guilds. Others see their primary contribution in the classroom, more specifically, in the lives of students. These educators apply their effort, time, and talent to the craft of teaching as a way to create transformative learning experiences. They are more focused on meeting the learning and developmental needs of students than on their own scholarly and institutional contributions. Still others believe that the ultimate value of their work should be experienced in the ministries and the lives of parishioners in the churches served by their students. In this scenario, the desired outcome of an educator's contribution lies beyond the classroom in the lives of parishioners whom their former students will serve.

Although each of the approaches above has merit, each falls short of locating the rationale for theological education in the story of God's redemptive mission. In my experience, unfortunately, only a few theological educators gain their sense of rationale, purpose, and calling for their craft by locating it in the world, in our mission to point the world to Jesus. These educators believe that those who do not yet identify with the church and have not yet experienced the redeeming work of Christ are the ones who should experience and benefit from their work. In this understanding of their vocation, faculty members believe that the impact of their scholarship and teaching should move beyond the classroom through the church to a world in need of redemption.

Although each of the four approaches noted above creates value for different constituencies, an expansive vision of biblicism, crucicentrism, conversionism, and activism leads us to envision the fruit of our efforts bringing transformation beyond the scholarly community, our students, and the church, into the lives of those who have not yet tasted redemption. In this manner, theological education gains a compelling rationale in the very redemptive mission of God. With this sense of mission, theological educators find themselves engaged in something much bigger than their own careers and institutions: theological education for the sake of the world.

Theological education for the sake of the world demands curricular emphases and learning outcomes not often found in evangelical seminaries. With grounding in the social sciences and theology, missiological concerns and content should take a much more prominent and expansive role in all programs in order to help students and faculty members develop a theologically informed approach to cultural exegesis—the interpretation of a culture's assumptions, values, structures, artifacts, and behaviors. The propensity and skill to exegete culture so that we can create a credible and compelling witness to the risen Christ and his kingdom should inform every discipline in the theological academy and remind us of the mission and purpose established for us in the narrative of Scripture. In other words, we need to turn theological education inside out.

Turning theological education outward also means taking seriously Jesus's command to make disciples of all peoples. We are part of a global body of believers engaged in the most audacious mission ever attempted: the establishment of an enduring testimony of the risen Christ in every ethno-linguistically distinct people group. It's our privilege to be a part of that endeavor. How we engage in it is as varied as the magnificent diversity of the world's peoples. If the church is to be guided in its mission by the envisioned consummation of the reign of Jesus, then we must pursue its realization wholeheartedly and sacrificially. "After this I looked, and there before me was a great multitude that no one could count, from every nation, tribe, people and language, standing before the throne and before the Lamb. They were wearing white robes and were holding palm branches in their hands. And they cried out in a loud voice: 'Salvation belongs to our God, who sits on the throne, and to the Lamb'" (Rev. 7:9–10).

A vision of the community of believers as diverse as the world's peoples yet unified in their worship of the crucified, risen, and reigning Lamb of God is the most stirring testimony to the power of the gospel that we could ever imagine. It ought to drive us outward, moving beyond the comforts of our own cultural settings into places and among peoples whose way of life challenges our ethnocentrism, ignorance, and indifference to the plight of almost eight billion souls whom God loves, for whom Christ died, and with whom we share our broken planet.

The next evangelicalism, already present, already agitating for change, already creating a vision of the kingdom that transcends its theological and social inheritance, demands a theological education that courageously addresses our failures and shortcomings, rethinks and rearticulates our theological DNA, and grounds our presence in the world in the hope of the gospel. Creating and sustaining that kind of theological education will require a thickening of our theology and a quickening of our heart for the lost. Theological education for the sake of the world finds its rationale in engaging the needs of the world with the redemptive power of the gospel and the life-changing truth of Scripture. That's the hope of the gospel expressed in a theological education that matters to the world. That's a calling worth giving our lives to.

– Epilogue: Hope –

Dear Brett, Sofia, Anna, Justin, and Ellie,

The next evangelicalism is already here. You embody it in your yearning for our movement to ground its identity and mission squarely and solely in the hope of the gospel. Your privilege is to envision, create, and execute theological education that will redefine a movement in crisis. Your voices need to be heard, your vision needs to be seen, and your passion needs to be felt in an enterprise that all too easily privileges the status quo and resists becoming what it needs to be.

Don't give up. At times it will seem like the fog and din of the last fifty years of culture wars and partisan politics are impenetrable and all-consuming. But they're not. Most of the dominant voices creating that fog and din are fading. Age, irrelevance, and hypocrisy have lowered their volume, thinned their timbre, and gutted their credibility. Theological education for the next evangelicalism must shape, sharpen, and embolden new voices resolved to change the conversation about Jesus in the broader culture.

Don't be impatient but do be urgent. The next evangelicalism is already more expansive than most think, but it needs the grounding that theological education bathed in the hope of the gospel and turned inside out for the sake of the world can provide. It needs institutional heft and boost to bring diverse voices, prophetic voices, credible voices to the fore. It desperately needs theological depth *framed by the biblical story of redemption, focused on the Christ event, driven by a vision of the kingdom, and conversant with a skeptical world. You can provide that through a theological education that develops a richer and thicker understanding of the Bible, the cross, conversion, and mission.*

Don't spend too much time looking over your right shoulder, even though your most strident opposition will come from the right wing of the movement, those who bear the legacy of fundamentalism most proudly. Cruciformity calls you to love them, listen to them, and firmly keep moving forward with a vision for theological education that steps beyond some of the boundaries they feel the need to defend.

I envy you. I wish I could relive my life as a theological educator. That's not because I have a lot of regrets. In fact, the opposite is true. I live with deep gratitude for the privilege of living out my calling and my passion to see lives transformed by the gospel through over forty years as a theological educator. What a satisfying life—one that still humbles and amazes me. You embody my hope as an educator that somehow, in spite of all our flaws and foibles, in some small ways, perhaps as small as a mustard seed, those of us who have gone before can embolden and encourage those coming behind us to pursue their calling as a theological educator for the sake of the world and the hope of the gospel.

For you,

Mark

For Further Thought

Some questions:

- What institutional changes would be required to develop and deliver theological education for the sake of the world?
- How would the composition of a faculty and the expertise and calling of each faculty member need to change to create and deliver a curriculum organized around the grand narrative of Scripture with the cross as its axial theological theme, engaging the questions of the world and experiencing the presence of the Holy Spirit, with the primary goal of helping God's people create a credible and compelling gospel presence?
- How can seminaries convince leaders of the next evangelicalism of the relevance and power of theological education to shape the movement?

Notes

Preface

1. I have used pseudonyms to protect the privacy of these five leaders.
2. I am indebted to Dr. Soong-Chan Rah for introducing me to the phrase "the next evangelicalism." His book *The Next Evangelicalism: Freeing the Church from Western Cultural Captivity* (Downers Grove, IL: IVP, 2009) has profoundly shaped my thinking about evangelicalism and theological education. Although written over a decade ago, its prophetic voice and vision are even more needed in evangelicalism today.

Chapter 1

1. Unless otherwise indicated, Scripture quotations in this book come from the New International Version (2011).

Chapter 2

1. Some of the text in the next few paragraphs first appeared in Mark Young, "Recapturing Evangelical Identity and Mission," in *Still Evangelical? Insiders Consider Political, Social, and Theological Meaning*, ed. Mark Labberton (Downers Grove, IL: IVP Books, 2018), 46–65.
2. Molly Worthen, *Apostles of Reason: The Crisis of Authority in American Evangelicalism* (New York: Oxford University Press, 2014), 3.
3. D. G. Hart, *Deconstructing Evangelicalism: Conservative Protestantism in the Age of Billy Graham* (Grand Rapids: Baker Academic, 2004), 17.

4. Douglas A. Sweeney, *The American Evangelical Story: A History of the Movement* (Grand Rapids: Baker Academic, 2005), 23.

5. Notable contributions to this literature include Mark Noll's *American Evangelical History: An Introduction* (Malden, MA: Blackwell, 2001); Frances FitzGerald's *The Evangelicals: The Struggle to Shape America* (New York: Simon & Schuster, 2017); Molly Worthen's *Apostles of Reason*; and Randall Balmer's *Evangelicalism in America* (Waco, TX: Baylor University Press, 2016). Also see the five-volume work entitled *A History of Evangelicalism: People, Movements, and Ideas in the English-Speaking World*, ed. David W. Bebbington and Mark A. Noll (Downers Grove, IL: IVP Academic, 2018).

Chapter 3

1. David W. Bebbington, *Evangelicalism in Modern Britain: A History from the 1730s to the 1980s* (London: Unwin Hyman, 1989), 2–3.

2. Mark A. Noll, "Defining Evangelicalism," in *Global Evangelicalism: Theology, History, and Culture in Regional Perspective*, ed. Donald M. Lewis and Richard V. Pierard (Downers Grove, IL: IVP Academic, 2014), 20.

3. Richard J. Mouw, *Restless Faith: Holding Evangelical Beliefs in a World of Contested Labels* (Grand Rapids: Brazos, 2019), 6.

Chapter 4

1. See, for example, Frances FitzGerald, *The Evangelicals: The Struggle to Shape America* (New York: Simon & Schuster, 2017), 13; Thomas S. Kidd, *The Great Awakening: The Roots of Evangelical Christianity in Colonial America* (New Haven: Yale University Press, 2009); Mark Noll, *America's God: From Jonathan Edwards to Abraham Lincoln* (New York: Oxford University Press, 2005); Grant Wacker, *Heaven Below: Early Pentecostals and American Culture* (Cambridge, MA: Harvard University Press, 2001) and *America's Pastor: Billy Graham and the Shaping of a Nation* (Cambridge, MA: Belknap Press of Harvard University Press, 2014).

2. See Marilynne Robinson's excellent essay "Puritans and Prigs: An Anatomy of Zealotry," *Salmagundi*, no. 101/102 (Winter-Spring 1994): 36–54, https://www.jstor.org/stable/40548719.

3. Douglas A. Sweeney, *The American Evangelical Story: A History of the Movement* (Grand Rapids: Baker Academic, 2005), 17.

4. For a discussion of what these *solae* formulations have meant in

Hispanic communities, see Elizabeth Conde-Frazier's book in this series: *Atando Cabos: Latinx Contributions to Theological Education* (Grand Rapids: Eerdmans, 2021).

5. For an insightful exploration of the question of authority in American evangelicalism, see Molly Worthen, *Apostles of Reason: The Crisis of Authority in American Evangelicalism* (New York: Oxford University Press, 2014).

6. See Peter H. Wilson, *The Thirty Years War: Europe's Tragedy* (Cambridge, MA: Belknap Press of Harvard University Press, 2009).

7. See "Evangelicals and Catholics Together: The Christian Mission in the Third Millenium," *First Things*, May 1994, https://www.firstthings.com/article/1994/05/evangelicals-catholics-together-the-christian-mission-in-the-third-millennium.

8. Mark A. Noll, *The Civil War as a Theological Crisis* (Chapel Hill: University of North Carolina Press, 2006), 18.

9. Keith D. Stanglin and Thomas H. McCall, *Jacob Arminius: Theologian of Grace* (New York: Oxford University Press, 2012), 34. See also Th. Marius van Leeuwen, Keith D. Stanglin, and Marijke Tolsma, eds., *Arminius, Arminianism, and Europe: Jacob Arminius (1559/60–1609)*, Brill's Series in Church History, vol. 39 (Leiden: Brill, 2009).

10. See Mark Charles and Soong-Chan Rah, *Unsettling Truths: The Ongoing Dehumanizing Legacy of the Doctrine of Discovery* (Downers Grove, IL: InterVarsity Press, 2019).

11. Theodore Dwight Bozeman, *To Live Ancient Lives: The Primitivist Dimension in Puritanism* (Chapel Hill: University of North Carolina Press, 1988), 14. See also Matthew Bowman, "Primitivism in America," Oxford Research Encyclopedia, accessed February 23, 2021, https://oxfordre.com/religion/view/10.1093/acrefore/9780199340378.001.0001/acrefore-9780199340378-e-416.

12. Robinson, "Puritans and Prigs," 37.

13. Thomas S. Kidd, *Who Is an Evangelical? The History of a Movement in Crisis* (New Haven: Yale University Press, 2019), 29.

14. Roger E. Olson and Christian T. Collins Winn, *Reclaiming Pietism: Retrieving an Evangelical Tradition* (Grand Rapids: Eerdmans, 2015), 90.

15. Olson and Winn, *Reclaiming Pietism*, 182.

Chapter 5

1. Frances FitzGerald, *The Evangelicals: The Struggle to Shape America* (New York: Simon & Schuster, 2017), 13. See also Thomas S. Kidd, *The*

Great Awakening: The Roots of Evangelical Christianity in Colonial America (New Haven: Yale University Press, 2009), and Mark Noll, *America's God: From Jonathan Edwards to Abraham Lincoln* (New York: Oxford University Press, 2005).

2. See George Marsden, *Jonathan Edwards: A Life* (New Haven: Yale University Press, 2003); Robert Jenson, *America's Theologian* (New York: Oxford University Press, 1988); and Thomas S. Kidd, *George Whitefield: America's Spiritual Founding Father* (New Haven: Yale University Press, 2014).

3. Quoted in Iain H. Murray, *Jonathan Edwards: A New Biography* (Carlisle, PA: Banner of Truth Trust, 1987), 163–64, and cited by Douglas A. Sweeney, *The American Evangelical Story: A History of the Movement* (Grand Rapids: Baker Academic, 2005), 44.

4. FitzGerald, *The Evangelicals*, 18.

5. Thomas S. Kidd, *God of Liberty: A Religious History of the American Revolution* (New York: Basic Books, 2010), 22.

6. For a wonderful description of the power of testimony in worship, see Keri Day's *Notes of a Native Daughter: Testifying in Theological Education* (Grand Rapids: Eerdmans, 2021).

7. Kidd, *God of Liberty*, 55.

8. Kidd, *God of Liberty*, 9.

9. Mark A. Noll, "Revolution and the Rise of Evangelical Social Influence in North Atlantic Societies," in *Evangelicalism: Comparative Studies of Popular Protestantism in North America, the British Isles, and Beyond, 1700–1900* (New York: Oxford University Press, 1994), 118.

10. Mark A. Noll, *The Civil War as a Theological Crisis* (Chapel Hill: University of North Carolina Press, 2006).

11. Perry Miller, *The Life of the Mind in America from the Revolution to the Civil War* (New York: Harcourt, Brace & World, 1965), 47, cited in Noll, *The Civil War*, 21n15.

12. Noll, *The Civil War*, 20.

13. Steve W. Lemke, "The Uneasy Conscience of Southern Baptists: Support for Slavery among the Founders of the Southern Baptist Convention," *American Baptist Historical Society*, 2016, 254–70.

14. Noll, *The Civil War*, 73–74.

15. Jemar Tisby, *The Color of Compromise: The Truth about the American Church's Complicity in Racism* (Grand Rapids: Zondervan, 2019), 109.

16. Quoted in Edwin J. Blum, "Gilded Crosses: Postbellum Revivalism and the Reforging of American Nationalism," *Journal of Presbyterian History* 79 (2001): 290, and cited by Sweeney, *The American Evangelical Story*, 112.

17. Christian Smith with Michael Emerson et al., *American Evangelicalism: Embattled and Thriving* (Chicago: University of Chicago Press, 1998), 4.

18. See Albert J. Raboteau, *Slave Religion: The "Invisible Institution" in the Antebellum South*, updated ed. (Oxford: Oxford University Press, 2004), and L. H. Whelchel Jr., *The History and Heritage of African-American Churches: A Way Out of No Way* (St. Paul, MN: Paragon House, 2011).

19. Daniel O. Aleshire, *Beyond Profession: The Next Future of Theological Education* (Grand Rapids: Eerdmans, 2021), 56.

Chapter 6

1. *The Fundamentals: A Testimony to the Truth* (1910; repr., Chicago: American Theological Library Association, 1986), microfiche B4000; ATLA monograph preservation program, ATLA fiche 1986-0772, accessed at Yale Divinity Library.

2. Douglas A. Sweeney, *The American Evangelical Story: A History of the Movement* (Grand Rapids: Baker Academic, 2005), 165.

3. See Daniel O. Aleshire, *Beyond Profession: The Next Future of Theological Education* (Grand Rapids: Eerdmans, 2021), 55.

4. See Walter Rauschenbusch, *A Theology for the Social Gospel* (Louisville: Westminster John Knox, 1997; original New York: Macmillan, 1917), and Christopher H. Evans, *The Social Gospel in American Religion: A History* (New York: NYU Press, 2017).

5. David W. Bebbington, *The Dominance of Evangelicalism: The Age of Spurgeon and Moody*, vol. 3 of *A History of Evangelicalism: People, Movements, and Ideas in the English-Speaking World* (Downers Grove, IL: InterVarsity Press, 2005), 246–51.

6. See Matthew Avery Sutton, *American Apocalypse: A History of Modern Evangelicalism* (Cambridge, MA: Belknap Press of Harvard University Press, 2014). Dispensational premillennialism has remained a significant hermeneutical and theological presence in populist evangelicalism. The "Left Behind" series, sixteen novels based on dispensational premillennialist eschatology, had sold over 80 million copies as of 2018.

7. Geoffrey R. Treloar, *The Disruption of Evangelicalism: The Age of Torrey, Mott, McPherson, and Hammond*, vol. 4 of *A History of Evangelicalism: People, Movements, and Ideas in the English-Speaking World* (Downers Grove, IL: InterVarsity Press, 2017), 185.

8. The identity of the persecuted minority has been nourished among

evangelicals for generations in the "Lost Cause" narrative that greatly influenced Southern civil religion and, particularly, fundamentalism. See Charles Reagan Wilson, *Baptized in Blood: The Religion of the Lost Cause* (Athens: University of Georgia Press, 1980, 2009).

9. See Darren Dochuk, *From Bible Belt to Sun Belt: Plain-Folk Religion, Grass Roots Politics, and the Rise of Evangelical Conservatism* (New York: Norton, 2011).

10. Frances FitzGerald, *The Evangelicals: The Struggle to Shape America* (New York: Simon & Schuster, 2017), 147.

11. Grant Wacker, *Heaven Below: Early Pentecostals and American Culture* (Cambridge, MA: Harvard University Press, 2001), 11.

12. See Amos Yong, *Renewing the Church by the Spirit: Theological Education after Pentecost* (Grand Rapids: Eerdmans, 2020).

13. Sweeney, *The American Evangelical Story*, 172.

14. See Grant Wacker, *America's Pastor: Billy Graham and the Shaping of a Nation* (Cambridge, MA: Belknap Press of Harvard University Press, 2014).

15. FitzGerald, *The Evangelicals*, 192.

16. Carl F. H. Henry, "Why Christianity Today?," *Christianity Today* 1, no. 1 (October 15, 1956): 20.

17. Carl F. H. Henry, *The Uneasy Conscience of Modern Fundamentalism* (Grand Rapids: Eerdmans, 1947, 2003), 88–89.

18. Carolyn Renée Dupont, *Mississippi Praying: Southern White Evangelicals and the Civil Rights Movement, 1945–1975* (New York: New York University Press, 2013), 238.

19. Frances FitzGerald, *Cities on a Hill: A Journey through Contemporary American Cultures* (New York: Simon & Schuster 1986), 178, cited in FitzGerald, *The Evangelicals*, 285–86.

20. Susan F. Harding, *The Book of Jerry Falwell: Fundamentalist Language and Politics* (Princeton: Princeton University Press, 2000), 22, 286n25, cited in FitzGerald, *The Evangelicals*, 290.

21. Adam Laats, *Fundamentalist U: Keeping the Faith in American Higher Education* (New York: Oxford University Press, 2018), 244.

22. Timothy Larsen, "'War Is Over, If You Want It': Beyond the Conflict between Faith and Science," *Perspectives on Science and Faith* 60, no. 3 (September 2008): 148–52.

23. Worthen includes a letter written to ETS officers in 1965 by then secretary of the society, Vernon Grounds, that includes the following concern of a resigning member: "My own long acquaintance with fundamentalism (I grew up in it and, through the Society, have heard its expression for a long time) indicates that a remark to the effect that the 'inerrancy' which

is claimed for the Bible is really an inerrancy claimed for fundamentalist interpretations of it, is all too true." Molly Worthen, *Apostles of Reason: The Crisis of Authority in American Evangelicalism* (New York: Oxford University Press, 2014), 53.

24. Worthen, *Apostles of Reason*, 54.

25. Craig Blomberg, *Can We Still Believe the Bible? An Evangelical Engagement with Contemporary Questions* (Grand Rapids: Brazos, 2014), 131.

Chapter 7

1. Mark A. Noll, "Chaotic Coherence: Sola Scriptura and the 20th Century Spread of Christianity," in *Protestantism after 500 Years* (New York: Oxford University Press, 2016), 258–79.

2. See Christian Smith, *The Bible Made Impossible: Why Biblicism Is Not a Truly Evangelical Reading of Scripture* (Grand Rapids: Brazos, 2011, 2012).

3. For a fuller exploration of the Bible as a story, see my *One True Story, One True God: What the Bible Is All About* (Grand Rapids: Our Daily Bread Publications, 2021).

4. Jonathan Haidt, *The Righteous Mind: Why Good People Are Divided by Politics and Religion* (New York: Vintage Books, 2013), 328.

5. Lesslie Newbigin, *The Gospel in a Pluralist Society* (Grand Rapids: Eerdmans, 1989), 15, quoted in Craig B. Bartholomew and Michael W. Goheen, "Story and Biblical Theology," in *Out of Egypt: Biblical Theology and Biblical Interpretation*, ed. Craig Bartholomew et al. (Grand Rapids: Zondervan, 2004), 150.

6. Lesslie Newbigin, "The Bible: Good News for Secularised People" (keynote address, Europe and Middle East Regional Conference, Eisenach, Germany, April 1991), Newbigin Archives, University of Birmingham, 6. Cited in Michael W. Goheen, *The Church and Its Vocation: Lesslie Newbigin's Missionary Ecclesiology* (Grand Rapids: Baker Academic, 2018), 18n11. See further https://missionworldview.com/wp-content/uploads/2020/06/ea8a85_fa f8a6551b14431db8fd326cdc197c6a.pdf.

7. Lesslie Newbigin, *A Word in Season: Perspectives on Christian World Missions* (Grand Rapids: Eerdmans, 1994), 118.

8. See Jacques Ellul, *The Subversion of Christianity* (Grand Rapids: Eerdmans, 1986).

9. N. T. Wright, *The New Testament and the People of God* (Minneapolis: Fortress, 1992), 42.

10. Lesslie Newbigin, "The Centrality of Jesus for History," in *Incarna-*

tion and Myth: The Debate Continues, ed. Michael Goulder (Grand Rapids: Eerdmans, 1979), 200, cited in Goheen, *The Church and Its Vocation*, 23n27.

11. Goheen, *The Church and Its Vocation*, 45–46.

12. See Rom. 16:16; 1 Cor. 16:20; 2 Cor. 13:12; 1 Thess. 5:26; and 1 Pet. 5:14.

13. For a fuller exploration of these ideas, see my chapter, "A Necessarily Wary Enterprise: North American Evangelicals and Contextualization," in *Understanding Insider Movements: Disciples of Jesus in Diverse Religious Communities*, ed. Harley Talman and John Jay Travis (Pasadena, CA: William Carey Library, 2015), 317–32.

14. Daniel B. Wallace, "Introduction: Who's Afraid of the Holy Spirit? The Uneasy Conscience of a Non-Charismatic Evangelical," O Bible.org, December 1, 2005, https://bible.org/seriespage/introduction-whos-afraid-holy -spirit-uneasy-conscience-non-charismatic-evangelical.

Chapter 8

1. David Bebbington, "The Nature of Evangelical Religion," in *Evangelicals: Who They Have Been, Are Now, and Could Be*, ed. Mark A. Noll, David W. Bebbington, and George M. Marsden (Grand Rapids: Eerdmans, 2019), 52.

2. Fleming Rutledge, *The Crucifixion: Understanding the Death of Jesus Christ* (Grand Rapids: Eerdmans, 2015), 44.

3. "Annual Address to the Methodist Societies," in *Minutes of Several Conversations . . . of the People Called Methodists* (London, 1892), 374f., cited in David Bebbington, "The Nature of Evangelical Religion," in Noll, Bebbington, and Marsden, *Evangelicals*, 52.

4. Billy Graham, *Peace with God* (Garden City, NY: Doubleday, 1953).

5. Miroslav Volf, *Exclusion and Embrace* (Nashville: Abingdon, 1996), 298.

6. Rutledge, *The Crucifixion*, 611.

7. Rutledge, *The Crucifixion*, 566.

Chapter 9

1. John Newton wrote the lyrics to this hymn in 1772. It was originally published as hymn #41 in the *Olney Hymns*, 1779, 54.

2. See Stanley Grenz, *Theology for the Community of God* (Nashville: Broadman & Holman, 1994).

3. This material is excerpted from *One True Story, One True God: What the Bible Is All About* by Mark Young. Copyright 2021. Used by permission of

Our Daily Bread Publishing, Box 3655, Grand Rapids, MI 49501. All rights reserved.

4. End of excerpted material.

5. I am indebted to Brandon Washington for this insight.

6. Lesslie Newbigin, *The Household of God: Lectures on the Nature of the Church* (New York: Friendship Press, 1954), 8–9.

7. Millard Erickson, *Christian Theology*, 2nd ed. (Grand Rapids: Baker Books, 1998), 1026.

8. Bruce Hindmarsh, "Is Evangelical Ecclesiology an Oxymoron?," in *Evangelical Ecclesiology: Reality or Illusion?*, ed. John G. Stackhouse Jr. (Grand Rapids: Baker Academic, 2003), 15–38.

9. Lesslie Newbigin, *Word in Season: Perspectives on Christian World Missions* (Grand Rapids: Eerdmans, 1994), 118, cited in Michael W. Goheen, *The Church and Its Vocation: Lesslie Newbigin's Missionary Ecclesiology* (Grand Rapids: Baker Academic, 2018), 60.

10. Goheen, *The Church and Its Vocation*, 61–62.

Chapter 10

1. David W. Bebbington, *Evangelicalism in Modern Britain: A History from the 1730s to the 1980s* (London: Unwin Hyman, 1989), 3. For further development of this concept, see pp. 10–12.

2. Donald P. McNeill, Douglas A. Morrison, and Henri J. M. Nouwen, *Compassion: A Reflection on the Christian Life*, rev. ed. (New York: Doubleday, 1983), 120–21.

3. McNeill, Morrison, and Nouwen, *Compassion*, 120.

4. Lesslie Newbigin, *Truth to Tell: The Gospel as Public Truth* (Grand Rapids: Eerdmans, 1991), 90.

5. Lesslie Newbigin, *The Gospel in a Pluralist Society* (Grand Rapids: Eerdmans, 1989), 227.

6. Daniel B. Wallace, "Introduction: Who's Afraid of the Holy Spirit? The Uneasy Conscience of a Non-Charismatic Evangelical," O Bible.org, December 1, 2005, https://bible.org/seriespage/introduction-whos-afraid-holy-spirit-uneasy-conscience-non-charismatic-evangelical.

7. Michael W. Goheen, *The Church and Its Vocation: Lesslie Newbigin's Missionary Ecclesiology* (Grand Rapids: Baker Academic, 2018), 59.